Psychological Testing at Work

Books by Edward Hoffman

Available from McGraw-Hill:

Ace the Corporate Personality Test
The Right to Be Human: A Biography of Abraham Maslow

Additional works:

Future Visions: The Unpublished Papers of Abraham Maslow
The Drive for Self: Alfred Adler and the Founding of Individual Psychology
What to Study: 101 Fields in a Flash

PSYCHOLOGICAL TESTING AT WORK

**How to Use, Interpret, and Get the Most
out of the Newest Tests in Personality,
Learning Style, Aptitudes, Interests, and More!**

Edward Hoffman, Ph.D.

McGraw-Hill

New York   Chicago   San Francisco
Lisbon   London   Madrid   Mexico City   Milan
New Delhi   San Juan   Seoul   Singapore
Sydney   Toronto

McGraw-Hill

A Division of The McGraw·Hill Companies

1 2 3 4 5 6 7 8 9 0 AGM/AGM 0 9 8 7 6 5 4 3 2 1

ISBN: 0-07-136079-4

This book was set in Baskerville by North Market Street Graphics.

Printed and bound by Quebecor/Martinsburg

 This book is printed on recycled, acid-free paper containing a minimum of 50% recycled, de-inked fiber.

The purpose of this book is solely to acquaint readers with psychological assessment in global business today. The sample test items and scoring interpretations provided are not intended in any way to provide actual diagnostic, clinical, or managerial guidance for anyone who may read this book. Those in the workplace who are experiencing emotional difficulties, whether job-related or otherwise, are advised to see a licensed mental health professional immediately for accurate diagnosis and intervention.

To the memory of my teacher Edwin Karpf

Contents

Preface

This book has been germinating for a long time. Ever since my undergraduate days at Cornell University, and later as a doctoral student at the University of Michigan, I've felt the need for a popular overview of psychological testing. Only highly technical, dry, and often obtuse works existed. And while weighty volumes filled with thousands of references have periodically appeared, none have provided a clear, concise, and satisfying picture of what psychological tests—especially in today's workplace—are all about.

Why has this been so? Perhaps such a book wasn't absolutely necessary until now. As a recent adage has it, we've each become managers of our own careers in this new economy—where job security and promotion ladders have become as obsolete as typewriters and vinyl records. It's a situation that has developed not only in the United States, but increasingly in Japan, China, and European nations as well. But that's not all. Many managerial thinkers are declaring that the very notion of a personal "job" tied to a specific organization and involving a set of guaranteed benefits will soon be dead. Yes, men and women will continue to be "employed" in performing a myriad of necessary tasks—but no longer in the traditional sense of occupying stable, full-time positions for indefinite periods of time. That structure will be gone forever. Sound scary?

Well, the implications are clear. If information is indeed power, then to gain knowledge about our own interests, abilities, skills, and talents has never been more important. Psychological tests are crucial in precisely this domain. In the new economy, those who are ignorant about personality assessment—and what it means for their own career success—will find themselves badly at a competitive disadvantage, akin to "computer illiterates" and "computer phobics."

For as never before, psychological testing has become a major force in the workplace. From employee screening and preselection to managerial development and leadership training—and even in the emerging field of expatriate placement—tests are being utilized by organizations globally large and small. To understand testing design and purpose, strength and weakness, is no longer an intellectual luxury for curious employees; it's become essential for all of us.

And yet, few outside this scientific specialty know very much about it. Serving as an expert witness providing court testimony in the past few years, I discovered this fact personally. Much to my initial surprise, not only were the vast majority of otherwise well educated jurors unaware of the most basic features of cognitive and personality assessment, so, too, were most attorneys and judges. When, in the courtroom, I presented aspects of current test construction, scoring, usage, and interpretation, they were "all ears"—and from their interested appearance, clearly absorbing such information for the first time.

Such experiences convinced me to undertake this book. My goal has been to highlight some of the most important features of psychological testing in today's workplace—and in so doing, to help general readers become savvy about what this booming field is all about. Because it has become influenced—perhaps inevitably in today's society—by governmental legislation, regulation, and court decision making, I have also included up-to-date material on psychological testing and the law.

I hasten to emphasize that this book is hardly intended as exhaustive, but rather as a guide to a huge terrain of scientific theory, research, and organizational practice. The number of popular articles, professional journals, and books devoted to this topic is mounting almost exponentially, and to summarize accurately this body for laypersons, and not just managers or human resources professionals, is an important task.

Above all, I wish to focus on how personality tests—and their allied forms in biodata and interviewing—are actually applied in the real world of contemporary business. Far too often, arcane battles in the "ivory tower" have served only to confuse and mystify those who might truly benefit from a greater sophistication about this scientific realm; fortunately, matters are changing for the better in this regard.

If I have been able to create a meaningful and lucid portrait of psychological testing in today's workplace, then my goal for this book will have been fulfilled.

Acknowledgments

This book would not have been possible without the valuable help of others. Reflecting the focus of my professional career, I've planned for several years to write a general volume on psychological testing in the business world today. Thanks to the enthusiasm of my literary agent, Alice Martell, and the encouragement of my editors Susan Barry, Griffin Hansbury, Susan Clarey, and especially Yedida Soloff, at McGraw-Hill, this idea has finally become a reality.

For many hours of lively conversation related to this book's topics, I'm grateful to Fannie Cheng, Elena Estrin, Jack Fei, Paul Palnik, Dr. Sam Menahem, Dr. Russ Reeves, K. Dean Stanton, and Dr. Ted Mann. Professor Eric Freedman of Michigan State University has been a valuable source of legal erudition.

I wish to express my appreciation to Kathy Kolbe, president of the Kolbe Corporation, for her generous time and encouragement in my tackling the subject of conative assessment. My professorial colleagues Xu Jinsheng and Michael Bond in China, and Ichiro Kishimi, Shoji Muramoto, and Yoshikazu Ueda in Japan have helped broaden my cultural perspective.

For their conscientious research efforts, I am indebted to Harvey Gitlin, Linda Joyce, and Kyung-mi (Mia) Song. Above all, I wish to thank my family for unflagging good cheer and support, enabling me to finish this project successfully.

1

Today's Testing Boom

Though psychological testing has flourished for more than a century, it's been mainly valued for many years in clinical, educational, or research settings. Certainly, such assessment continues to occupy an important role in these fields. But as never before, a mounting number of organizations in the workplace are also relying upon testing to select and develop their employees.

In one such industry, where the cost of compensating well-trained professionals has skyrocketed, firms are increasingly screening job candidates' mental makeup—to be sure of making a wise investment. Managers all want to avoid a revelation scant months after the hiring that the new, seemingly terrific employee lacks "the right stuff" to be successful; selecting the wrong person can be a costly mistake indeed.

In a major *New York Times* article, an organizational psychologist active in this industry recently noted, "I'm doing pre-employment screening for banks on candidates who are going to make $20,000 a year—why not do the same for companies that are going to spend millions on those they think will be on their team for a long time?"

To an extent that would have seemed unthinkable not long ago, these job applicants must take a detailed cognitive battery that measures their learning aptitude, as well as their capacity to apply something learned to a new situation. But there's much more than that. Most are now also subjected to personality testing in order to determine their conscientiousness, anger proneness, stress-coping ability, willingness to obey directives, vocational interests, and attitudes related to coworkers, customers, and the general public.

Applied by psychological experts familiar with this particular industry, such tests require candidates to answer *true* or *false* to questions including, "I think I would like the work of a dress designer," "Sometimes, I feel like smashing things," and "Women should not be allowed in cocktail bars." Whether responding to a well-known, broad test like the Personality Factor (16PF), which measures traits like aggressiveness and competitiveness, or a specially developed instrument used by several major companies in this industry—each applicant generates a statistically derived profile: some result in hiring, and others prompt rejection. Of course, there's no opportunity for appeal.

Despite what test instructions soothingly advise, there are certainly right answers and wrong answers to personality items, just as for cognitive items; and failing a personality measure used in employee screening typically has only one outcome; this is true for virtually all organizations that use them.

How do the job candidates themselves view this process? As might be expected, some quietly grumble and make derisive remarks during the test-taking procedure. As for applicants who refuse to submit to psychological testing and probing interviews—and it's not as rare as you might think—can they still be hired? After all, don't companies in this industry have other, more performance-related factors to utilize in making their decisions?

Increasingly, the answer is no. Executives and managers have found testing extremely valuable, particularly in tapping subtleties, that no other tool provides. With a growing trend as well for using psychological consultants in team building, stress management, and other organizational matters once applicants are already aboard, the likelihood of reverting back to the pretesting era is nil.

In short, this industry has jumped on the testing bandwagon in a big way. Now admit it, you didn't know that the National Football League was so enamored with this once-arcane scientific field, did you?

Psychological assessment in today's workplace is booming. Though annual surveys reporting corporate usage show year-to-year variability—depending partly, perhaps, on economic factors—current evidence indicates that from fully one-third to over one-half of all major companies rely upon such measures, particularly for pre-employment screening, staff development, team building, and management and leadership training. While personality tests have been used in industries such as insurance and law enforcement for over 80 years, the field is rapidly expanding. At all levels, more and more workers are likely to face a personality test at some point, perhaps a critical one, in their careers. Why is this happening?

For one thing, there's been a dramatic improvement in the tests themselves. Mathematical breakthroughs in combination with advanced computer technology have made these measures far more powerful statistically than in the past. As a result, these can much more accurately differentiate highly desirable job candidates from those highly unappealing, and all those in between.

Second, the tests are much improved conceptually. Dating back to the influence of physician Sigmund Freud nearly a century ago, many personality measures were derived from theories on human development that are now as obsolete as record players and slide rules. Swayed by the Freudian notion of infant sexuality, such measures were filled mainly with items probing bodily functions and impulses, incestuous fantasies, and deeply buried childhood conflicts.

The Blacky Test from the 1950s was among the most notorious. Based entirely on Sigmund Freud's ideas, it required people to respond to drawings of Blacky the Dog in arguments, tensions, and sexual longings relating to his doggy-family members. Presumably, the stories that individuals told in response to these unwittingly bizarre pictures would reveal significant aspects about their own personality. Likewise rooted strongly in Freudian theory, more clinically, widely used measures like the Rorschach inkblot test and the Minnesota Multiphasic Personality Inventory also aimed at uncovering deep-seated emotional strains.

Not surprisingly, such tests had little value for employers concerned with far more practical matters: which job applicants and employees were most likely to steal or embezzle, frequently show up late or call in sick, ignore directives, or openly defy their supervisors? Conversely, these instruments offered meager aid in identifying the *best* workers: those among their peers who ought to be groomed and promoted into supervisory, managerial, or executive positions within the organization.

As late as the mid-1970s, many researchers doubted whether psychology would ever be of genuine help to firms seeking a reliable way to hire and promote employees. It's no coincidence that polygraph usage soared in corporate usage, as it seemed to offer a more scientific approach to the workplace than represented by the Rorschach or Blacky tests. All of that, however, has changed dramatically in recent years; for as we'll see in chapters 2 and 3, sophistication in the personality field has been amassing steadily.

A third factor in the current importance of psychological assessment is the emergence of computers, which has made test scoring, and even administering, much more user-friendly. Increasingly, within seconds after an applicant completes his or her cognitive or personality battery via a computer hookup to the Internet, the answers are tabulated and scored, and a detailed profile is printed out for the interviewer. Based wholly on the candidate's responses—whether involving mathematical problems, reading comprehension, or attitudes about fistfights or income tax cheating—the profile is even accompanied with specific recommendations: *hire, do not hire,* or *maybe hire.*

On this basis, the interviewer can proceed quickly to the next step in the often costly hiring process: welcoming the candidate into the personnel office for a detailed interview and related job discussion—or, instead, politely offering the verbal kiss of death, "Thank you for coming today. We'll be in touch with you soon."

To a degree that would have seemed startling not long ago in the workplace, nowadays, electronic psychological screenings are often conducted in the applicant's own home—via a push-button phone and/or fax. For instance, the *Wall Street Journal* recently highlighted a Florida psychology company that conducts honesty testing entirely over the phone. This may well represent the wave of the future: job applicants for various firms must call a toll-free number from home at a prearranged time and respond instantaneously in yes or no format to prerecorded questions that assess their integrity. For example, a job candidate might have 5 seconds to press either a 1 (for yes) or a 2 (for no) to items such as, "Should an employee be fired for taking home a small item, like a stapler?" or "If you found a bag of money on the street, would you try to find the owner?" or "I have sometimes felt like hitting a supervisor at work." As the company's chief psychologist commented wryly, "We're not looking for people who need to spend a lot of time deciding how to answer such questions."

Fourth, in our increasingly fast-paced and technologically driven society today, businesses are finding themselves obliged to rely on psychological tests in the absence of other worthwhile data. For instance, it has become standard for employers to refrain from providing character references on current or past employees due to fear of litigation should they prove incompetent or dishonest at the new position. Organizations are also worried that a disgruntled employee might sue for defamation. Precisely in an era when companies are more eager than ever for information about their candidates' talents, skills, character weaknesses, and potentialities, it's no longer available from the workplace itself.

Whereas in the past, employers could readily gain references on qualities like the candidate's dependability, diligence, hotheadedness, or trustworthiness—such data through employment references are now virtually nonexistent. The enactment by the U.S. Congress of the Employee Polygraph Protection Act of 1988 has likewise removed another useful source of psychological data for many employers, particularly in the private sector where lie detector usage is most severely restricted. For precisely this reason, facts gleaned from individual testing today can be important, even crucial, in making the right hiring decision.

Finally, personality measures have proven helpful in the crucial spheres of management and leadership training. Though such assessment isn't yet as widespread or well developed as that used in preemployment screening, growing corporate demand for such instruments is likely to change this situation quickly. In an era when employee retention, especially in high-technology and allied fields, is now among the highest organizational priorities, not only in the United States but in Europe and Asia as well, such training has become a significant enterprise. To maximize its effectiveness, many firms are utilizing standardized personality tests.

For example, the Myers-Briggs Type Indicator (MBTI), which we'll examine in chapter 7, has proven especially popular in recent years, particularly in management training and team building. Based on the type theory formulated by psychiatrist Carl Jung more than a half-century ago, this test alone generates annual sales of $3.5 million for its publisher. Indeed, the sheer financial size of the contemporary testing industry demonstrates the seriousness with which businesses and governmental organizations are taking psychological assessment. In a word, they are cost-effective, especially in screening out highly undesirable potential workers.

Certainly, most executives and upper-level managers know that these tests are fallible, but statistics and probabilities justifiably carry a lot of weight. In certain areas of performance, such as employee productivity or theft, it's possible to calculate rather specifically the direct financial benefit versus cost of psychological assessment. For instance, the Seattle-based department store chain Nordstrom, Inc., uses the Reid Survey, a well-known measure that screens job applicants for violent tendencies, drug use, and dishonesty. The paper-based test takes just 15 minutes to complete and is immediately fed through a scanner to obtain results. When Nordstrom recently conducted a controlled test of 400 applicants at one store, it tracked the results from the Reid Survey: approximately 100 weren't recommended but were hired anyway. Three months later, more than double from the do-not-hire category had left the company, compared with those who had scored in the test's desirable range.

Managers and executives also know that there are indirect benefits to reap, such as reducing the likelihood of litigation arising from the hiring of incompetent, dishonest, or potentially violent workers. Consequently, cognitive and personality tests are increasingly used in hiring for many types of positions, and are prized for other situations ranging from team building to executive development.

In short, it's hardly surprising that industries like the National Football League have climbed aboard the testing bandwagon. As the tests themselves grow in conceptual and methodological power, it's even becoming possible to predict organizational efficiency and profitability based on the data that such tests generate. For example, there's now quantifiable evidence that placing people with compatible emotional or problem-solving traits together can improve or accelerate the synergy of their work teams; conversely, teams with other worker "mixes" are almost doomed from the start to ineffectiveness or outright failure.

Does this mean that days are coming when we'll be able to predict the NFL championship, the Rose Bowl, or the next team to win the World Series in baseball—based on players' personality test data? Maybe. In this regard, if you know anyone planning a professional football career—or one in banking, insurance or investment, hospitality or lodging, retail or business-to-business sales, manufacturing, transportation, and a growing list of other industries including service and health care—they'd certainly benefit from knowing what psychological testing is all about.

And that's the subject of this book.

2

What Is Personality?

"You've got a great personality!" is a prize compliment to receive, and might well make our day. But what does it really mean? How about the warning that a new coworker has definite "personality problems?" Should we start worrying? Where does our personality come from, anyway? What accounts for the striking differences in temperament we see among individuals, even among closely related family members?

At what age do children start showing distinctive traits? Do men and women actually possess different qualities when it comes to love and intimacy—or honesty or achievement, for that matter? In addition, can we truly change aspects about ourselves that we dislike or want to improve, or is that goal just a lot of wishful thinking?

For more than a century, such fascinating questions have occupied the scientific study of *personality*, typically defined as the unique and enduring bundle of motivations and needs, attitudes, and behavioral tendencies that makes each of us who we are. On that point, there's little professional disagreement. But the issue of what creates, sustains, and changes personality has been hotly debated for generations. Fortunately, with the growth of developmental and biological psychology, we're now much closer to finding definite answers.

For more than 50 years, Sigmund Freud was the dominant figure in shaping both psychiatric and popular approaches to personality. From the turn of the twentieth century, when Freud published *The*

Interpretation of Dreams, until long after his death in advanced old age in 1938, he exerted an unprecedented influence. Originally trained in laboratory physiology at the University of Vienna (his early career was marked by seminal research on the electric eel), Freud was among the first medical and academic professionals to explore human personality in all of its complexity. Relying almost exclusively on information gleaned from his treatment sessions with patients, he developed an immense theoretical system called *psychoanalysis.*

As early as the 1890s, Freud became convinced that all young children experience sexual feelings for their parents (he termed this *infant sexuality*) and insisted that how such feelings are resolved is the structure through which our personality becomes formed for a lifetime. In particular, Freud emphasized the role of the mother as having overwhelming importance in this process: through such biologically related activities as feeding, bathing, toileting, stimulating, and soothing their infants, mothers determined how secure or insecure (i.e., "neurotic") their offspring would become. Freud had almost nothing to say about fathers—or siblings, relatives, peers, schools, or other wider cultural forces for that matter—in affecting personality development.

From about 1902 to 1912, Freud's two most important colleagues were the Viennese physician Alfred Adler and the Swiss psychiatrist Carl Jung. Both younger, but likewise brilliant and charismatic intellectual figures, they eventually broke with Freud because of his refusal to abandon the theory of infant sexuality as the key to human personality. In their viewpoint, Freud had given the world many insights regarding the human psyche, such as the existence of unconscious feelings, memories, and motivations; however, they regarded as nonsensical his view that every child experienced parentally oriented sexual desires. First Adler in 1911, and then Jung the following year, bitterly ended all relations with Freud to spearhead their own psychological schools of theory and treatment.

Adler's system became known as *individual psychology.* Its hallmarks were his concepts of the *inferiority complex,* the *spoiled child, sibling rivalry,* and *adult lifestyle*—all highly influential terms that he coined. Outgoing and effervescent with a masterful speaking ability, Adler won many supporters in applied fields because of his optimistic approach. Unlike the cynical, aloof Freud whom he came to dislike sharply, Adler believed that psychological insights could improve schooling, family life, and the workplace, and even abolish war and poverty.

Emphasizing child guidance, parent training, and teacher education as the three pillars for a better society, individual psychology achieved a peak influence during the 1920s and 1930s, particularly in Western Europe, but also in the United States, where Adler eventually resided until his death in 1937.

Like his adversary Freud, Adler was essentially a clinician with little interest in quantitative personality research, and even less in test development. Nevertheless, individual psychology under Adler generated many useful theories and therapeutic techniques, and has sustained a small but active international presence to this day.

Carl Jung, who was closer emotionally to Freud than Adler ever was (the two men traveled alone together to the United States in 1909 as guest lecturers at Clark University), was the son of a Protestant minister. Throughout an international career that lasted until his death in 1961, Jung relied strongly on mythology and fairy tales, comparative religion, and even mysticism in advancing his view of personality. He regarded spiritual feelings and needs as basic to human nature, yet also valued experimental design.

Jung devised one of the earliest, effective personality instruments: the *word association test* ("If I say *mother,* what's the first word that comes to your mind? Now, how about the word *father?*"), and later, provided the theory and personal encouragement that led to the creation of the Myers-Briggs Type Indicator, which we'll examine later in chapter 7. Ironically, though Jung's immense body of work was long rejected by American psychologists as soft-minded due to his spiritual viewpoint, the Myers-Briggs has brought Jung recognition as a major historical figure in applying personality theory to the workplace.

Though certainly differing in their specific notions, Freud, Adler, and Jung all argued that personality is formed by the age of six, greatly resists change thereafter, and is almost wholly caused by parenting, particularly maternal. This perspective became known as *psy-chodynamic*, referring to dynamic or changeable qualities within us emotionally.

The psychodynamic approach long dominated the fields of psychiatry, psychotherapy, counseling, social work, child guidance, and even cultural anthropology and criminology. Its broader influence, however, on American child rearing became immense due to the impact of one man: pediatrician Benjamin Spock. His *Baby and Child Care*, in its first year of publication in 1941, was an immediate success through sheer word of mouth, and it became a veritable bible for millions of parents through the 1960s. It spawned many imitative books whose message continues to permeate the Sunday newspapers and airwaves. Eventually translated into dozens of languages, *Baby and Child Care* presented the psychodynamic view in simple, persuasive terms: that our adult personality is almost entirely the product of how we're treated as young children by our parents.

The Freudian Gospel, as it came to be known, may have strongly affected American culture, but it never held much power in academic psychology. Rather, that status belonged to the behaviorist school, founded by John B. Watson. First at the University of Chicago and then, after moving to Johns Hopkins University in 1908, Watson emulated Russian neurologist Ivan Pavlov by studying reflexive behavior in animals. Following research on how rats learn mazes, Watson studied imitative behavior in rhesus monkeys and the homing mechanism of Florida terns. His campaign for *behaviorism*, as he termed it, began in 1913 with an academically famous "manifesto" that urged the establishment of a new psychology based solidly on rigorous and objective laboratory methods.

Two years later, Watson initiated a long-term study of children's development. Building a special observation chamber in a Washington, D.C., hospital, he analyzed how mothers and their infants interacted from birth onward. In highly influential research, he claimed that babies could be conditioned just like Pavlov's dogs. For instance, Watson could easily make a young child terrified of a rabbit by banging loudly whenever the rabbit was put near the youngster. Triumphantly, Watson demonstrated that he could also reverse this process by reintroducing the rabbit gradually and at a distance, under more gentle circumstances. Such work signaled that a new form of mental cure was possible.

During these years, Watson won a huge following among academic psychologists. In essence, he argued that human personality was almost entirely the product of conditioning associated with positive reinforcement (reward) and negative reinforcement (punishment); in this respect, people were as susceptible to behavioral shaping as white rats or birds. Watson further insisted that aside from simple reflexes and physiological drives for hunger or thirst, humans have no intrinsic personality: everything about us from shyness to extraversion, musical sensitivity to verbal prowess, is caused by externalities involving conditioning.

Because of scientific advances today, this view is probably even less scientifically tenable than Freud's psychoanalytic system, but it enjoyed overwhelming academic support for decades. Within major university departments, conditioning was a bedrock of psychological study. Indeed, it wasn't until the growth of biological psychology in the 1990s that behaviorism, as initially espoused by Watson and then by leading protégés like Clark Hull and B. F. Skinner, was finally knocked off its academic perch.

After a sexual scandal at Johns Hopkins wrecked Watson's academic career, he resourcefully landed a position with the J. Walter Thompson advertising agency in New York City. On the strength of innovative, successful marketing techniques, Watson quickly rose to executive rank; during the 1920s, mass advertising was just beginning to be established, and Watson taught an eager generation of business managers that people buy products in order to satisfy emotional rather than utilitarian needs.

Despite Watson's wealth and status in the advertising world, he felt intellectually isolated among his business colleagues. He therefore continued to write actively, and in 1924, his popular book, *Behaviorism,* was published. It promulgated his confident position: "Give me a dozen healthy infants, well-formed, and my own specified world to bring them up in and I'll guarantee to take any one at random and train him to become any type of specialist I might select—a doctor, lawyer, artist, merchant-chief, and yes, even into beggar-man and thief."

Watson's major bestseller, *Psychological Care of Infant and Child*, appeared in 1928. Sarcastically dedicating his book to "The first mother who brings up a happy child," he argued that parents had virtually unlimited capacity to create their child's personality: knowing how to administer the right mixture of reward and punishment was paramount. Though behaviorism quickly waned from the public eye with the onslaught of the Great Depression, it held sway in academic psychology for many decades thereafter. Sometimes, it was misportrayed or oversimplified in Psychology 101 courses. For example, America's leading behaviorist, B. F. Skinner, in old age confided to me that he had never really believed that humans lack higher values, needs, and goals; rather, he had only been suggesting that these arise from early conditioning and are subject to reinforcement just as are the physiological drives for food and water.

The third main school of human personality was founded by motivational theorist Abraham Maslow. Raised in Brooklyn, he studied both freudianism and behaviorism at the University of Wisconsin; after earning his doctorate in experimental psychology there in 1935, Maslow returned to New York City, and for several years, conducted research and taught psychology at Brooklyn College while learning informally with Alfred Adler.

It was after spending a summer's fieldwork among the Blackfoot Native American tribe that Maslow began articulating his own personality approach: namely, both the psychodynamic and behaviorist views were partly correct, but more important, all human beings possess a biologically based "core" of needs, goals, values, satisfactions, and frustrations.

Thus, in an unpublished 1938 report to the Social Science Research Council following his fieldwork, Maslow asserted, "It would seem that every human being comes at birth into society not as a lump of clay to be molded by society, but rather as a structure which society may warp or suppress or build upon . . . I am struggling now with a notion of a 'fundamental' or 'natural personality structure'."

During the next 5 years, Maslow developed his now-famous theory of the *hierarchy of inborn needs*. Emphasized internationally today in management and marketing, as well as psychology and counseling, Maslow's view was that people in all cultures share the same innate needs for safety and security, belongingness, esteem and respect, love, and self-actualization, and that these exist within an unfolding hierarchy. With the publication of his landmark work, *Motivation and Personality*, in 1954, Maslow at Brandeis University steadily gained guru status in the budding fields of managerial theory and organizational development.

Widely sought as a lecturer and consultant by innovative corporations, as well as governmental agencies, until his death in 1970, Maslow stressed the importance of fulfilling the higher, creative needs of men and women in the contemporary workplace. Reflecting his early career interests, Maslow was also a strong advocate for personality assessment. His influential approach (highlighted in chapter 11 of this book) is known as *humanistic* for its stress on uniquely human motivations and goals.

Biological Psychology

The humanistic approach articulated so forcefully by Maslow and his supporters has been buttressed by a fourth, and most recent, approach to personality: that of *biological psychology*. Drawing strongly from physiology and genetics, it has produced a convincing body of evidence that our emotional makeup—strengths, weaknesses, and even personal values and attitudes—is significantly shaped by biological forces. In this regard, biological psychology not only refutes the freudian view that parenting, especially mothering, overwhelmingly determines the child's lifelong personality, but the behaviorist baby-as-blank-slate position as well. For originating with empirical research by Stella Thomas and Robert Chess at New York University more than a quarter-century ago, a scientific consensus has emerged that innate factors broadly known as *temperament,* contribute at least 50 percent to our permanent adult personality.

The field of temperament is still quite young, but it's now possible to state that personality differences are apparent as early as birth. Even newborns exhibit great variability on such dimensions as reactivity, intensity and quality of mood, exploratory behavior, ease of "warming up," adaptability, and sociability. Over the past decade, longitudinal studies have shown that these temperamental differences have important predictive value.

For instance, babies who are less adaptable seem to become teens and adults with higher anxiety; similarly, babies who seek out new stimuli like sounds and lights grow into adults who become easily bored and seek more novelty in their daily lives. Traits like achievement motivation, self-confidence, and the risk-taking characteristics of entrepreneurship have now become measurable by kindergarten and the lower elementary school grades, as are dimensions such as sociability, or what psychologists call *introversion-extraversion.* Though the evidence is far from conclusive, there's a growing scientific view that such qualities are physiologically and genetically influenced.

Among the leading innovators in biological psychology today is Dr. Robert Cloninger of the Washington University Medical School. Rather than focusing on infants and children, he has devoted nearly 15 years to identifying the biological underpinnings of adult personality. In his system, there are seven distinct dimensions, vital to understanding the functioning of normal men and women, as well as those diagnosed with a wide variety of psychiatric disorders. These encompass four dimensions that Dr. Cloninger refers to as *temperament* [involving (1) harm avoidance, (2) novelty seeking, (3) reward dependence, and (4) persistence] and three he specifies as *character* [involving (5) self-directedness, (6) cooperativeness, and (7) self-transcendence]. Whereas *temperament* is seen to involve mainly lower, physiological aspects that are strongly genetically influenced, *character* involves higher cognitive processes, as well as attitudes and values, that are affected by social learning and the environment. Dr. Cloninger has argued forcefully that this model provides a fresh way of understanding the strikingly different ways that people behave in daily life.

To this end, Dr. Cloninger and his colleagues have developed a personality test known as the Temperament and Character Inventory (TCI). Issued in 1994 by the Center for Psychobiology of Personality at Washington University, the TCI has been internationally applied in clinical and research settings. It comprises 125 items involving the aforementioned 7 major scales of personality and 25 subscales.

Though the TCI has been used chiefly in diagnostic analysis, it seems to have definite workplace potential as well. In particular, the TCI subscales measuring shyness with strangers versus gregariousness, disorderliness versus regimentation, impulsivity versus reflection, and empathy versus social disinterest, all have obvious relevance for job performance in a wide variety of settings.

As long as we're on the subject of biological psychology, is there really a gene for selfishness, altruism, shyness, or extraversion? How about sexual orientation or sexual drive? At the current stage of psychology research, the answer seems to be a clear-cut no. Despite what the Sunday newspapers proclaim, genetics has found no such evidence. Rather, as Dr. Cloninger and others have recently concluded, genetic influence on personality comprises an additive or cumulative effect of many different genes, all interacting with one another—and with our social environment, including parents, siblings, peers, teachers, and mass media—in ways that are extremely complex, and certainly not well understood at the present time.

Does Our Personality Change?

The notion of personality change is central to the applied fields of counseling, psychotherapy, executive coaching, and management and leadership training. Many different approaches to personality change exist, but they all insist that growth, reeducation, and new learning during adulthood are possible. This viewpoint has recently gained physiological validation, as psychotherapy with obsessive-compulsive disorders have been found to produce measurable and permanent changes in the human brain; the psychotherapeutic treatment of post-traumatic stress disorder is likewise showing demonstrable physiological benefit.

Nevertheless, psychologists also believe that it becomes more difficult for us to change our personality as we age; when change does happen, it's almost invariably a modification, instead of a huge alteration, of our inner "core." Consequently, today, applied fields aim mainly at helping the individual function better in terms of *who he or she is,* rather than attempting a total makeover.

So if you're basically shy and introverted, it's unlikely that a management training program will try transforming you into someone who enjoys leading work teams. Rather, the goal might be to help you better understand extraverts and recognize your own pattern of functioning vis-à-vis other people. Similarly, when it comes to teaching "emotional intelligence" or social skills, the trend is to identify employees' specific job-related behaviors, and ways to improve them—not to try an overall personality transformation.

Interestingly, within the field of *psychometrics* (i.e., psychological testing), this perspective has also been empirically supported. That is, while people's scores on personality tests do show changes over time to an extent, most psychologists attribute such changes largely to flaws in the reliability of the tests, rather than to actual changes in the individual's personality. Overwhelmingly, the consensus is that personality is permanently "fixed" by late adolescence and that it changes minimally through the span of adult life. Unless intervention is involved—and the older we get, the more difficult it is to change—each person remains his or her core self.

Not long ago, many theorists contended that major life events can impact significantly upon individual personality. But after contradictory data emerged, the revised notion has become: whenever we experience a major upheaval (e.g., marriage or divorce, a big promotion or a sudden job loss, a long-distance relocation, or a child's birth), this is always mediated by our basic personality. These events never exert the same impact on everyone the same way.

For instance, imagine a train derailment disaster in which a carload of people suffers significant injuries. One individual may be traumatized and feel confirmed, as a victim, that life is unpredictable and dangerous; another will experience the same event as a minor inconvenience; and still, a third may socialize with nursing staff and develop a close friendship as a result.

In short, therefore, substantial agreement exists that our personality remains stable throughout life and resists major change. Indeed, many philosophers have declared that people fear change more than any other aspect of life, and in the specialties of counseling and psychotherapy, such *resistance* as it's called has been recognized for 100 years.

What's the single personality trait most difficult to change? No, it's not our degree of honesty, reliability, emotional openness, or ambition, though these don't exactly shift from day to day. Up-to-date research suggests that it's our degree of extraversion or outgoingness. And this makes logical sense from our experience: while a true extravert can certainly force himself to spend a workday at home alone, reading departmental documents, he won't enjoy such solitude. Similarly, an introvert can be induced to chair a boisterous sales conference, but she'll find it unpleasant and seek time by herself as soon as possible.

For extraversion, even more than other identifiable personality traits, it seems that people revert to being who they really are once external pressures are removed. And maybe that's a good thing. At any rate, that people become "stuck in their ways" is a true observation throughout the world. Ambitious, conscientious, orderly, extraverted, honest, even-tempered, risk-taking—or not—essentially, we are who we are. Scientific personality study has many unanswered questions, but that much is clear.

3

A Brief History
of Workplace Testing

Reliance upon psychological tests for hiring and promotion may be booming today, but it's a scientific field that is more than a century old. Few outside the specialty of psychometrics are much acquainted with it. But knowing, even from a bird's-eye view, this significant history helps us to understand present developments a lot more clearly.

Psychometrics dates back to the eminent Sir Francis Galton of England, who in 1884 used a dictionary to demonstrate that human personality comprises a specific number of groupable traits. For example, words like *cheerful, jovial, merry,* and *mirthful* encompass a quality embodying happy sociability, whereas *sad, downcast, gloomy,* and *melancholy* constitute a different cluster. However, Galton's research was largely theoretical and had little impact on business.

It was in 1915 that personality study was first put to major real-world usage, when the Carnegie Institute of Technology established a Division of Applied Psychology, and the following year, a Bureau of Salesmanship Research. By then, the field of psychology had emerged from its childhood and had become increasingly more rigorous experimentally and statistically. The Bureau was created to sponsor research aimed at scientifically selecting salespeople through personality testing. It was in 1916, too, that the first American police department made use of psychological tests in the hiring process. Probably more than any other industry, law enforcement has relied upon these instruments to identify suitable and unsuitable job candidates. After all, a hotheaded or impulsive salesperson may kill a profitable deal, but a quick-tempered police officer may harm a real human being. As the latest newspaper headlines reveal, accurately pinpointing such potential misfits remains a vital social issue.

United States involvement in World War I hastened the growth of psychological testing, for the military required measures that could be administered rapidly to large numbers of potential soldiers. These focused on intelligence and were the earliest of their kind to assist in personnel selection. With John Otis and Robert Yerkes among the key test developers, hundreds of thousands of recruits were assessed with the Army Alpha (the main instrument) or the Army Beta (a nonverbal test for illiterates and nonnative English speakers).

However, the number of actual selection decisions that were based on these tests remains unclear. Individual bases varied considerably in their support for the testing enterprise and in their reliance on test results for screening and classifying recruits. Nevertheless, the huge amount of data collected by Otis, Yerkes, and their colleagues heightened interest in using intelligence tests for selecting candidates in private industry.

In addition to creating group tests of general intelligence, the U.S. Army during World War I pioneered a series of so-called trade tests to assess specific job knowledge and skills. These were devised to differentiate the men tested into four groups of proficiency: (1) novices, (2) apprentices, (3) experienced, and (4) experts. The tests themselves generally fell into three basic categories: (1) verbal and (2) picture tests (both using paper-and-pencil measurement of job knowledge) and performance tests (which generally involved hands-on use of job-related machinery).

Perhaps, more important, American involvement in World War I spurred the development of the first standardized personality test, the Woodworth Personal Data Sheet (also called the Woodworth Test of Emotional Stability). During the war, the Woodworth Personal Data Sheet was administered to recruits for the purpose of screening for additional psychiatric evaluation—those recruits most likely to "crack" during actual combat and, therefore, unfit for military induction.

In 1919, after the war was over, the Committee on Classification of Personnel, associated with the U.S. Adjutant General's Office, instituted a program of personality data collection to aid in deciding officer furloughs. Former employers' ratings of officer character traits, such as leadership and trustworthiness, were gathered and used as a decision tool.

Personality tests during World War I were used mainly to identify recruits emotionally unsuited for combat, but professional interest in tests to predict job performance grew swiftly. By the close of the war, for instance, rating scale methods of personality assessment, popularized by the military and the Bureau of Salesmanship Research, were already being used by several personnel consulting firms and companies to predict job success.

The majority of researches, however, knew that existing personality theory and methodology were still too primitive to develop really effective tests. As Yerkes commented in 1920, "Methods at once simple and reliable are not yet available. It is nevertheless obvious that personality attributes are as important as intelligence for industrial placement and vocational guidance." In particular, Yerkes and his colleagues were concerned about problems caused by the *halo effect,* in which, for example, a popular employee is given inflated ratings by his or her supervisor on features of job performance that have nothing to do with the target trait being measured (e.g., detail-mindedness or reliability). This type of error is notorious in education, where teachers often give higher grades, especially on subjective exams like essays, to their favorite students.

During the 1920s and early 1930s, an emphasis on refining test methodology brought several new paper-and-pencil personality measures to the workplace. Seeking to assess specific traits, these included Gordon Allport's Ascendance-Submission Test (assessing self-esteem or dominance) and the Bernreuter Personality Inventory, which was an all-in-one measure of six scales that combined assembled items from previously devised scales, including Allport's.

The Bernreuter proved particularly useful in predicting the performance of salespeople, as well as those of nursing students and factory supervisors. Interestingly, though, managers typically found such tests disappointing in failing to identify those likely to stand out as either the best or the worst employees. Consequently, many researchers urged caution in relying too heavily on psychological tests in making hiring decisions.

The 1940s saw the Minnesota Multiphasic Personality Inventory (MMPI) emerge as a leading personality test—a status it held undisputed for ensuing decades. Comprising over 500 questions and a variety of subscales, including an innovative *lying scale* to determine if the job applicant was grossly exaggerating his or her personality strengths. During World War II, the Cornell Science Index provided the equivalent of the Woodworth Personal Data Sheet to screen out emotionally unstable recruits.

The use of personality testing in the workplace grew steadily in that period. For instance, the Life Insurance Sales Research Bureau sought to measure specific personality traits related to performance by life insurance salespeople; such qualities as self-confidence were assessed in conjunction with a personal history measure. In another series of studies, the Bureau explored the personality traits apparently linked to successful sales ability. Similarly, in the 1940s, the Sears Company commissioned psychologist Robert Thurstone to create a procedure for selecting executives. The resulting test battery included the Guilford Martin Personality Inventories (revised in 1949 as the Guilford and Zimmerman Temperament Survey) as well as ability and interest measures. Sears screened more than 10,000 job applicants by means of such personality tests.

Another key test developer was Abraham Maslow, who later pioneered the field of motivational psychology. In the late 1930s and 1940s, Maslow developed both the Social Personality Inventory and the Security-Insecurity Inventory, instruments for assessing such factors as self-esteem, dominance, and adaptability. Like most of such instruments, though, these were mainly used in clinical and research, rather than business, settings. Nevertheless, Maslow had a strong interest in applying psychological insights to industrial practice, and first began doing so for his brothers' cooperage business in the 1940s.

United States entry into World War II accelerated the growth of standardized testing. Many leading psychologists, as well as those who would gain prominence in the postwar years, worked hard together in helping to defeat Nazi Germany. They devised ability tests to select and classify thousands of military personnel in the Army, Navy, Army Air Force, and the Office of Strategic Services (OSS). Never before had it been feasible to move so quickly through cycles of job analysis, creation of ability tests, evaluation of test validity and reliability, and refinement of procedures. It's not surprising, therefore, that so much progress was made in both the methodology and application of testing.

World War II definitely proved a watershed in legitimating the use of psychological tests in the workplace. Managers and executives affirmed their value, and surveys revealed that by the mid-1950s nearly two-thirds of large firms were using personality and interest tests in employee selection. But academicians continued to voice caution about the worth of such instruments. For one thing, a proliferation of tests due to organizational needs led to many measures of doubtful reliability and validity. Although these appeared to satisfy organizational objectives, most rested on paltry theory. Similarly, university researchers expressed concern about the use of tests like the MMPI in predicting worker achievement or productivity, rather than in merely screening for emotional stability. Typically, psychologists argued that there were too little scientific data to justify such empirical leaps. As two prominent psychologists insisted in 1965, "The best that can be said is that in some situations, for some purposes, some personality measures can offer helpful predictions."

The advent of President Lyndon Johnson's "Great Society" legislative program marked the usage of personality tests in employee selection to unprecedented levels. However, all that began to change rapidly due to a barrage of criticism that such tests were racially and ethnically discriminatory, unreliable, and easily faked. As highlighted in the next chapter of this book, the Civil Rights Act of 1964 and the creation of the Equal Employment Opportunity Commission (EEOC) to enforce its workplace applicability severely challenged the worthiness of employment testing. Subsequent U.S. Supreme Court decisions in the 1970s laid out the circumstances under which the use of testing for personnel selection and promotion would be permitted, and the nature of validation evidence that firms would be required to prove in the event of a legal challenge to a particular test's use. Afraid of long and costly legal challenges, many companies immediately started curtailing their reliance on personality testing in favor of interviews and the polygraph.

Consequently, the use of personality testing in the workplace declined sharply for all but the most sensitive positions, such as police officers, firefighters, air traffic controllers, and nuclear plant operators. For these kinds of jobs, personality tests like the MMPI, the Thematic Apperception Test, Rorschach Inkblot Test, and the Edwards Personal Preference Scale were widely used in employee screening.

In the 1970s, personality testing also came under fuselage from psychological theorists. Certainly, new instruments like the Myers-Briggs Type Indicator (based on psychiatrist Carl Jung's theory of personality type) came into vogue, and prominent thinkers like Abraham Maslow advocated more extensive types of assessment, including efforts to uncover employees' higher motivations and goals. But many others condemned the whole psychometric field as misguided, and even questioned whether we really have stable, enduring personalities at all. As a doctoral student at the University of Michigan in those days, I can well remember the obvious absurdity of such contention.

Personality testing in America had hit the doldrums, and the entire notion of using tests to screen job candidates was on the defensive. But a rebound was inevitable. Slowly, in the late 1980s to early 1990s, a new model for understanding human personality began to emerge at respected research centers. It cohered around a five-factor approach, which argued that almost all normal human personality could be understood in terms of five overall dimensions: (1) neuroticism, (2) extraversion, (3) conscientiousness, (4) agreeableness, and (5) openness to experience.

Ironically, by emphasizing the study of human personality in terms of commonly used adjectives like *outgoing, diligent, amiable,* and *artistic,* the *Big Five model*—as it's now called—strongly follows the viewpoint of Sir Francis Galton, who trailblazed the field of personality study more than a century ago. Perhaps predictably, perhaps not, we've definitely come full circle back to the starting point of speculation about our inner world.

The Big Five model has not only proven appealing to academicians, but has also generated a large volume of empirical research showing its value in many settings, including the business world. For example, psychologists have found the Big Five model useful in helping to predict those who will benefit most from counseling, adapt best to expatriate managerial life, or display greatest sales ability. A variety of studies have shown, too, that the Big Five approach is valid for assessing people in widely varying cultures, such as China, India, Japan, the Philippines, Turkey, and South America.

Intriguingly, there's evidence that Asians have a sixth major constituent of normal adult personality usually absent among Occidentals, which researchers call *filial piety.* This is a trait that encompasses dutiful feelings and actions toward one's parents and other respected elders, and that is distinct from the other five personality dimensions.

It would be foolish, of course, to deny that the Big Five model has its critics. Some psychologists have argued that none of the five scales measure such major traits as creativity, inventiveness, or the capacity to resist conformity. Others have insisted that the Big Five model has no place for spirituality, religiosity, or transcendence— values that are highly important for some people's lives, and that may well be biologically or genetically mediated. However the legitimacy of such criticisms, the Big Five model has become so influential that it now strides like a giant across the entire field of personality assessment. It may be premature, but some theorists are already suggesting that the Big Five will eventually give way to yet another model, rooted in human biology and temperament, that is truly global in scope.

Before concluding our history of psychological assessment in the American workplace, it's useful to highlight a rather different approach: that involving the lie detector, or polygraph. First used by police interrogators and investigators in 1924, it gained dominance in business settings where employee misconduct was frequent and its impact likely to be severe. Indeed, until recently, it was the preferred method for identifying problems of theft, alcohol and drug use, sabotage, and violence. Lately, due to governmental fears about nuclear secrets and their theft at research facilities, the polygraph is suddenly gaining renewed appeal.

As a popular icon in modern American culture, the lie detector has long been associated with Hollywood movies and dime novels, a prop for tough-talking detectives and defiant gangsters, but the reality has always been more mundane.

The polygraph instrument simultaneously measures blood pressure and pulse, sweat gland activity, and respiratory patterns. Before the advent of latest technology, a pneumographic tube was typically fastened around the subject's chest, and a blood pressure–pulse cuff strapped around the arm. Although the current polygraph is standardized as to the physiological measures obtained, the actual examination process can vary tremendously, depending on who conducts the investigation. The questions asked, the physiological responses to which are recorded, can vary widely—and so, too, can the methods by which various sources of data are combined to reach the final conclusion.

For this reason, lie detector testing is often regarded as much as a consequence of the examiner's skill and experience as it is of the instrument itself. Certainly, it's this subjective element, as well as the perceived history of employer misuse, that gave polygraph testing a controversial reputation almost from the outset.

During the 1960s and 1970s, lie detectors became a common pre-employment screening device. Private employers used lie detectors to screen job applicants, as well as to investigate wrongdoing in the workplace, especially theft. And, as employee theft began soaring in that socially stormy period, reliance upon polygraphs correspondingly mounted. Ironically for privacy advocates today, while many other psychological screening measures in the 1970s were criticized as racially or ethnically biased, lie detectors raised no such objections. Specifically, these were viewed as objective instruments that lacked the seemingly discriminatory features of intelligence and personality tests. During the heyday of the civil rights era, therefore, many firms shifted from psychological tests to the polygraph as a way to avoid potential lawsuits.

Thus, a 1978 study in *Personnel* reported that one-quarter of major U.S. corporations were using lie detectors for three key purposes: (1) to verify employee applications, (2) to conduct periodic assessments of worker honesty, and (3) to investigate specific instances of theft or irregularities. By far, the largest percentage (almost 90 percent) of the companies that used polygraphs did so for the latter purpose.

By 1985, researchers estimated that more than one-half of the country's retail businesses, and over 30 percent of Fortune 500 companies, were using lie detectors. Indeed, one study at the time reported that polygraph-related lawsuits had become more numerous than those pertaining to employee discrimination. Critics increasingly argued that in the hands of nongovernmental agencies, the polygraph in America had become a dangerous instrument that pervasively violated individual privacy rights.

Such criticisms were hardly new. As early as 1959, Massachusetts became the first state to restrict lie detector testing; during the ensuing 30 years, roughly one-half of the states established at least minimal limitations. Generally, those states with strong union activity were much more likely to restrict workplace usage of polygraphs than those where unions were weak.

In the late 1980s, both the Office of Technology Assessment of the U.S. Congress and a task force of the American Psychological Association issued highly negative reports on the use of polygraphs. For instance, the U.S. Office of Technology Assessment concluded that, "There is at present only limited scientific evidence for establishing the validity of polygraph testing. Even where the evidence seems to indicate that polygraph testing detects deceptive subjects better than chance . . . in specific-incident criminal investigations, significant error rates are possible, and examiner and examinee differences and the use of countermeasures may further affect validity."

Coupled with growing public unease about the device in business settings, the effect of these combined sources spurred Congress' passage of the landmark Employee Polygraph Protection Act of 1988. Almost immediately, American companies shifted their focus to psychological tests in response to this Act; the situation remains unchanged today.

It's important to know that Congress was concerned mainly about the threat that polygraphs posed to employee privacy and job security, and not about the devices' accuracy or usefulness. How so? Because Congress specifically exempted from the Act those positions for which it considered lie detectors to be more crucial: specifically, jobs involving national security and defense, FBI contractors, providers or security services, and those with access to controlled substances. All other private job applicants were protected from lie detector testing.

Also, by allowing the limited use of lie detectors on existing private employees, Congress again chose a situation in which accurate information was most essential. That is, companies were permitted to use polygraphs for ongoing investigations of misconduct involving controlled substances or "economic loss or injury to the employers' business, such as theft, embezzlement, misappropriation, or an act of unlawful industrial espionage or sabotage." Not coincidentally, these are precisely the types of situations in which lie detector tests can be used most accurately, for under these circumstances, employers are most likely to have special information known to the perpetrators but not to other workers.

Congress acted further to protect employee privacy by limiting the kinds of questions that could be asked when lie detector use was allowed. For instance, examiners were prohibited from asking questions regarding certain specific topics, including political or religious belief or affiliation, or matters relating to sexual behavior. Likewise, examiners were restricted from posing questions in a manner designed to degrade, or necessarily intrude on, examinees.

Among the other important provisions of the Employee Polygraph Protection Act of 1988 are that examinees must be provided with an opportunity to review all questions to be asked during the test, and that examiners are barred from adding any other questions onto this list. Besides mandating these external controls on lie detector testing, Congress authorized examinees the right to stop the procedure at any time, and to be informed in writing if any other people would be observing the test, or if any other devices, such as a hidden camera, recorder, or two-way mirror, would be used. Finally, posttesting privacy was protected by limiting access to polygraph test results.

By the way, how accurate actually are lie detectors? Though in response to the apparent theft of nuclear secrets from its research centers, the U.S. Department of Energy has authorized a massive program of employee polygraph testing, many psychologists remain skeptical about its effectiveness and regard the claims of the polygraph industry (typically offering accuracy figures of 98 or 99 percent) as wildly inflated. In a recent study by the American Psychological Association, psychologists estimated lie detector validity at only 61 percent and strongly felt that results should not be admitted as evidence in court.

Especially in view of America's long-standing love affair with technology, it seems unlikely that the polygraph will disappear any time soon from the workplace. Rather, it's likely to maintain a continued presence for at least the foreseeable future. And who knows what breakthroughs in assessing human physiological response—perhaps in conjunction with remote computer databases and instrumentation—are just over the horizon?

The field of personality assessment has never been static, and undoubtedly, the new millennium will see additional change. By all indicators, such testing will only increase in importance through the coming years. So in managing our career advancement, the more we know about psychological testing, the greater likelihood of our success.

4

Testing and the Law:
What You Need to Know

Psychological testing in the workplace today is significantly impacted by the law. To an unprecedented extent, test developers and their corporate users alike are affected by civil rights legislation, federal regulations, and key court decisions. If you think, however, that employee privacy is the paramount issue in all this activity, guess again: it actually holds little import for the judicial system and for those involved with test creation and application—at least, as yet.

Rather, the two key subjects that dominate employer interest, as well as caution, about assessment are *negligent hiring* (and its cousin, *negligent retention*) and *adverse impact*. Virtually every company must now steer a course between these countervailing polarities, though more broadly, legalities sway how tests are created, implemented, scored, and interpreted. It's important for managers, human resources professionals, and organizational consultants to be acquainted with this domain, because it's pertinent to nearly every facet of employee assessment.

It's a truism that law in America is never static—an observation that is especially apt for labor issues. Nevertheless, over the past 15 years, such a formidable consensus has emerged on psychological testing that a major legal departure appears unlikely for the forseeable future; the ground seems solid indeed. Despite this clarity of legal consensus, keep in mind that what follows is still a broad picture and is decidedly not intended as a substitute for professional legal advice. When confronted with specific questions pertaining to assessment, it's vital to obtain the opinion of an attorney who specializes in this domain. Labor law is a well-established field, and knowledgeable attorneys aren't hard to find.

Key Federal Legislation and Rulings

Federal law and regulation of workplace testing stands on three pillars: (1) Title VII of the Civil Rights Act of 1964, (2) Equal Employment Opportunity Commission (EEOC) guidelines, and (3) the Americans with Disabilities Act. Let's look briefly at each in turn before focusing on the four key federal cases in this realm.

1. *Title VII of the Civil Rights Act of 1964.* Enacted by Congress on 2 July 1964 and amended in 1972 and 1991, this Act is the bedrock of employee rights concerning all matters of discrimination. Among its applicable provisions, the Act states:

   It shall be an unlawful employment practice for an employer to hire or to discharge any individual, or otherwise to discriminate against any individual with respect to his compensation, terms, conditions, or privileges of employment, because of such individual's race, color, religion, sex, or national origin; or (2) to limit, segregate, or classify his employees or applicants for employment in any way which would deprive or tend to deprive any individual of employment opportunities or otherwise adversely affect his status as an employee, because of such individual's race, color, religion, sex, or national origin.

   The courts have consistently interpreted this provision to mean that psychological tests must be free from any feature that could negatively affect an individual because of his or her race, gender, ethnicity, national origin, religion, and more recently, sexual orientation. Known in employment law as *adverse impact,* this provision greatly affects how tests are developed and standardized; more on adverse impact will be discussed later in this chapter.

2. *The U.S. Equal Employment Opportunity Commission (EEOC).* Established by Title VII of the Civil Rights Act of 1964, the EEOC began operating in 1965, and currently has an annual budget of over a quarter-billion dollars. It exists to promote equal opportunity in employment through administrative and judicial enforcement of federal civil rights laws, as well as offer education and technical assistance. Currently operating out of its headquarters in Washington, D.C., and 50 field offices, the EEOC in 1966 issued its first guidelines on employment testing, stipulating that all written tests must be *validated* (i.e., scientifically proven to measure what they claimed to measure).

    In 1970, the EEOC issued additional guidelines, not only more specific and technical, but also broadening the definition of *test* to include "all formal, scored, quantified or standardized techniques of assessing job suitability including specific qualifying or disqualifying personal history or background requirements, specific educational or work history requirements, scored interviews, biographical information blanks, interviewer's rating scales, and scored application forms."

    However purposeful, the EEOC's stipulations on employee testing were little known until they were applied by the U.S. Supreme Court in two key decisions: (1) *Griggs v. Duke Power Company* (1971) and (2) *Albermarle Paper Company v. Moody* (1975). These catapulted the EEOC's guidelines into legal prominence, adding to a host of antidiscrimination regulations promulgated by other governmental agencies, and finally morphed into the multiagency *Uniform Guidelines on Employee Selection Procedures.*

    The *Uniform Guidelines on Employee Selection Procedures* was adopted on 25 August 1978 by the EEOC, the U.S. Civil Rights Commission, and the Departments of Justice and Labor. Though interagency bickering about fine points had stalled final agreement for several years, the *Uniform Guidelines* (as known for short) marked a broad governmental consensus. Today, they're still very much in effect, and occupy a central position in how courts approach the issue of employee testing.

But the EEOC's focus on testing didn't end there. In 1982, it importantly affirmed, "It shall not be an unlawful employment practice for an employer . . . to give and to act upon the results of any professionally developed ability test provided that such test, its administration or action upon the results is not designed, intended or used to discriminate because of race, color, religion, sex or national origin."

The EEOC constructed this supportive language to permit the use of psychological testing—even those might inadvertently discriminate against certain groups, such as minorities— if an instrument's *job relatedness* was demonstrable. Through court decision relying upon the EEOC's own words, *job relatedness* is established "by professionally acceptable methods that the results are predictive of, or significantly correlated with, important elements of work behavior which comprise, or are relevant to the job or jobs for which candidates are being evaluated."

3. *The Americans with Disabilities Act (ADA).* Signed into law by President George Bush on 27 July 1990, the ADA prohibits discrimination based on disability in private sector employment, public accommodations, transportation, public services, and communications. The ADA defined disability as:

    1. Having a physical or mental impairment that substantially limits a major life activity
    2. Having a record of such a disability
    3. Being regarded as having such a disability

Employment discrimination, as recognized by the ADA, encompasses a broad spectrum of employment activities and policies, including recruiting and hiring, training and promotion, rates of pay, job assignments, leaves of absence, fringe benefits, and social programs.

Concerning recruiting and hiring of personnel (employment aspects today that often include psychological testing) the ADA specifically bars discrimination against *qualified* individuals with disabilities. Under the ADA's terms, men and women are *qualified* (i.e., identifiable as disabled) *if they can perform the essential functions of a job with or without reasonable accommodation.*

Not unexpectedly, the ADA didn't precisely define what *accommodation* meant, but it's understood to include such matters as making the workplace accessible—or modifying work schedules, equipment, training materials, examinations, and policies.

It's useful to know that in May 1994 and October 1995, the EEOC issued new regulations, derived from ADA guidelines, on preemployment interviewing. Essentially these broadened the ability of employers to ask preemployment questions related both to disability and reasonable accommodation. Attempting to clarify the circumstances under which such questions are acceptable, the new EEOC guidelines specifically allowed employers in the recruitment and hiring process to inquire about an applicant's need for accommodation, to ask about accommodation of applicants with obvious disabilities, and to question applicants who voluntarily reveal a disability or a need for accommodation in job performance.

As we'll see more closely in chapter 6, the ADA prohibits interviewers from asking questions that might elicit information about disabilities, and also stipulates that employers can require a job candidate's medical examination only after making a conditional offer of employment. However, employers are allowed to ask preemployment questions related to an applicant's ability to perform specific, job-related functions.

In addition, the ADA requires that a psychological test be administered in an accessible location and in a format accessible to those with disabilities. Such a stipulation is designed to make sure that a particular test is actually measuring a required skill, instead of the individual's disability.

Landmark Court Rulings

The past 30 years have witnessed four key cases related to psychological testing in the workplace. In combination, they exert a strong influence on the field today. Let's examine each in chronological turn.

1. *Griggs v. Duke Power Company (1971).* In this case decided by the U.S. Supreme Court, the Duke Power Company had organized one of its generating facilities into five departments, one of which, the labor section, paid substantially lower wages than the others. Duke Power established the requirement that, in any department other than the labor section, it would be necessary for new employees to hold a high school diploma and to achieve a certain minimum score on both a professionally developed general intelligence test and a similarly developed mechanical comprehension test. Also, while Duke Power Company did allow blacks to enter the highest-paying sections, it based promotional decisions on job seniority rather than on company security.

    Former employees at Duke Power filed suit and claimed they had suffered racial discrimination as a result of psychological testing. Relying strongly on the EEOC's 1970 guidelines, the Supreme Court found that Duke had made no effort to validate its use of these tests (i.e., to determine whether individuals' scores were measurably associated with job performance), and that adverse impact was clearly in evidence. In applying the notion of adverse impact to the use of psychological tests for the first time, the Supreme Court broke major ground in Griggs by affirming that discrimination hinges on the result, not the intent, of an employer's acts.

2. *Abermarle v. Moody (1975).* Similar to *Griggs v. Duke Power Company,* this U.S. Supreme Court case also centered on adverse impact. More vigorously and thoroughly, however, the court in Abermarle wrestled with the following issue: what must an

employer do to demonstrate the job relatedness of a psychological test that it administers to job applicants?

The facts in Abermarle were very similar to those of Briggs. In the mid-1950s, the Abermarle Paper Company in North Carolina began modifying its production lines by adding newer and more sophisticated machinery. Concurrently, it began requiring its employees in departments that used the complicated machinery to have a high school diploma; at the time, positions on these "skilled" lines were limited to white workers. Over the ensuing years, the company learned that its diploma requirement had failed to improve production quality; therefore, it added a new selection method: namely, psychological testing.

Such assessment involved two instruments that respectively measured verbal intelligence and mechanical comprehension: the Wonderlic Personnel Test and the Revised Beta Examination. However, as was true for its diploma requirement, the company neglected to conduct a formal study to discern whether its new employee selection method actually resulted in the hiring of more capable workers. Perhaps due to inertia, Abermarle never eliminated its high school diploma requirement, either.

By 1964, the company had begun allowing black employees to transfer to the skilled lines, provided they could "pass" the tests. Very few did. For this reason, and others related to the company's seniority system, a group of present and former black employees in 1966 filed suit against the owners of the paper mill, alleging that the company's employment practices had resulted in discrimination against them.

The Duke Power Company hadn't even attempted to determine whether the job skills inferences it had made on the basis of tests were accurate. But the Abermarle Paper Company, going to trial in mid-1971, was aware of Griggs, having been decided several months before. Though Abermarle had never before expressly considered the accuracy of the employment decisions it had made based on psychological tests, it now began such an undertaking on the eve of its appearance in district court.

Abermarle's executives hired an industrial psychologist to conduct a validation study. Spending a half-day at the plant, he devised a *concurrent validation* study, conducted by plant officials without his supervision. Relatively high-level employees, almost all of whom were white, took the two tests and their results were compared with their job performance, as rated by their supervisors. After examining all of the data gathered by Abermarle's management, the psychologist it had hired concluded that test performance was, indeed, related to job performance and that the instruments were valid.

However, relying heavily on the EEOC's previously obscure 1970 guidelines, the U.S. Supreme Court found a variety of deficiencies in Abermarle's validation study, and ruled on behalf of the plaintiffs. Among the Court's findings was that the job performance ratings used by supervisors were too vague, and therefore, "There was no way to determine whether the criteria actually considered were sufficiently related to the Company's legitimate interest in job-specific ability to justify a testing system with a racially discriminatory impact."

Two landmark cases have focused in part on the issue of employment testing and individual privacy. In *McKenna v. Fargo* (1978), the U.S. District Court for the District of New Jersey ruled on a law suit brought by plaintiff Robert McKenna and four other former job applicants (and represented by the American Civil Liberties Union) against Nicholas Fargo, director of Public Safety for Jersey City. Having all applied for the job of fire fighter, the plaintiffs claimed that intrusive psychological tests in the hiring process violated their constitutional rights to freedom of belief and privacy.

Psychological testing had begun in 1966, after race rioting in many New Jersey communities raised officials' concerns in racially charged Jersey City that its police and fire fighters be emotionally fit to withstand intense stress. Initially, job applicants were administered only the Minnesota Multiphasic Personality Inventory (MMPI) and a clinical interview by the psychological company hired by Jersey City; but by 1972, when plaintiff McKenna was 25 years old, they were additionally required to take the Rorschach inkblot test, the Thematic Apperception Test (TAT), the Edwards Personal Preference Scale (EPPS), the Draw-a-Person Test, and a nonstandardized Incomplete Sentences Test.

Following the clinical interview and test battery, the psychological firm issued a detailed report on the applicant's personality on five specific dimensions: the ability to (1) adjust to close community living, (2) follow orders, (3) withstand stress, (4) take calculated risks, and (5) be free of potentially detrimental fears (e.g., fear of heights or enclosed spaces). The report concluded with a specific recommendation of either: accept for hire, reject for hire, watch during probation, or refer for psychiatric help. At no time did Jersey City personnel ever see the raw scores of job applicants, but rather just the finished report.

In affirming for Jersey City, the court found no merit at all in the plaintiffs' claim that psychological testing had violated their right to religious belief. True enough, a few test items on the MMPI and EPPS related to belief in God, political opinions, and similar matters; however, the court found no evidence whatsoever that job applicants had been targeted for either employment or rejection on the basis of their religious or political viewpoints. Rather, "The evaluation was made for the purpose of selecting firemen who had a high probability of withstanding the psychological pressures of fighting fires and living in close quarters. The behavioral potentials which [resulted in hiring] recommendation were obviously relevant psychological and emotional factors, and not an orthodoxy of faith or political belief."

As to the issue of whether psychological testing violated the plaintiffs' constitutional right to privacy, the court found greater significance. In essence, it stated that "the constitutional protection afforded privacy interests is not absolute. State interests may become sufficiently compelling to sustain State regulations or activities which burden the right of privacy. Specifically, the highly stressful and dangerous nature of fire fighting allowed Jersey City to utilize intrusive psychological tests in the hiring process. "Because fire fighting, like police work, involves life-endangering situations, the State interest is of the highest order. Plaintiffs lose sight of the fact that a fireman who loses emotional control endangers his own life as well as those of other firemen. When a psychological evaluation intrudes on an applicant's privacy, it may save him from the risk of losing his life."

The most recent landmark case involving psychological testing was *Soroka v. Dayton Hudson Corporation* (1991). In a case with wide repercussion decided by the California Court of Appeals, First District, plaintiffs were former security guard applicants at Dayton Hudson's Target department stores. They claimed that having to undergo psychological testing in the hiring process violated their privacy rights, the Fair Employment and Housing Act, and the California Labor Code.

Prior to the lawsuit, Dayton Hudson had been using psychological testing for several years to screen out prospective security guards unwilling to follow directions or established rules, as well as those with addictive or violent tendencies who might put coworkers or customers at risk.

The company's goal was certainly reasonable, and the particular test was PsychScreen, a recently devised combination of the MMPI and the California Personality Inventory (CPI). Both measures, of course, have long been among the most widely respected in clinical psychology and psychiatry. But, just as McKenna and the American Civil Liberties Union had argued more than a decade earlier in New Jersey, plaintiffs' attorneys in California insisted that such tests contain illegally personal questions involving religious and political attitudes, and sexual activity.

In the Soroka case, privacy advocates were more successful. In reaching its decision, the court held that the standard used under California law to determine if a job applicant's privacy had been invaded was a *compelling interest* standard, the same as that used for a current employee. Although Dayton Hudson had a legitimate interest in hiring emotionally stable employees as security guards, the court held that it lacked a sufficiently compelling interest to justify the use of this particular measure.

Moreover, following the legal reasoning central to *Griggs* and *Abermarle*, the Soroka court found that Dayton Hudson had failed to demonstrate that a link existed between its test questions and the applicants' expected job duties. In other words, it had failed to prove sufficient test validity.

Subsequently, in 1996, a trial court in California banned the employment use of PsychScreen as a violation of the state's constitutional right to privacy and also of statutory prohibitions against preemployment inquiries concerning religion and sexual orientation. Dayton Hudson eventually agreed to settle the lawsuit by paying more than $2 million to the 2500 applicants who took the test.

And that's where matters stand now regarding major court decisions and employment testing.

Seven Key Legal Questions and Answers

1. *What is negligent hiring?*   It used to be that negligent hiring claims were filed only by employees who had been injured by a coworker. While a customer could sue if a job poorly done proved damaging in some way, the public had little recourse against employers for other kinds of harm committed by an employee. Now, however, many courts hold employers liable for injuries that employees inflict on anyone while on the job. Companies are expected to know enough about their employees' mental qualities to avoid trouble, and can be held liable for punitive damages as well as medical bills, lost wages, and the like. The stakes can be substantial: a Maryland jury recently awarded a plaintiff $2 million in a negligent hiring case.

The fundamental issue is whether the employer has taken reasonable precautions to avoid hiring people who might pose a significant risk to others in the job that's being filled.

The courts have consistently ruled, therefore, that employers must obtain a detailed history of the applicant's background, in order to avoid liability due to negligent hiring. Such information is typically gathered from biodata and the interviewing process, and employers who fail to obtain it are running a considerable legal risk. Hence, the current boom in background security checking, as well as in psychological testing. What employers can—and cannot—legally ask job applicants will be highlighted in chapter 5.

As never before, employers are being held liable for negligent hiring because their workers were improperly trained; lacked adequate experience; were mentally or physically disabled; were often intoxicated, forgetful, inattentive, or careless; or had a discoverable history of horseplay, recklessness, or maliciousness.

The expanded liability for negligent hiring has meant that employers increasingly use psychological tests to screen out potentially dangerous, dishonest, or unstable employees. For many types of jobs, especially in law enforcement or security work, an organization's failure to administer appropriate tests is a sure prescription for liability involving judgment of negligent hiring.

This doesn't mean that a firm must conduct a major investigation before hiring anyone. Several courts have ruled that no obligation exists to inquire routinely into an applicant's criminal record—and some state and local laws prohibit it. Rather, a company's duty is simply to recognize that its degree of care varies with the job at issue. The more intimate contact an employee will have with customers or the public, the more care that's necessary.

2. *What is negligent retention?* This legal notion is quite similar to that of negligent hiring: A company bears liability for the harmful actions of its employees if it failed to exert reasonable super-

vision, management, or intervention. Generally, the issue of psychological testing has occupied a much smaller place in this legal domain than in negligent hiring. Why? Because if the hiring process, including the use of personality tests, is successful, then misfits and hotheads are unlikely to become employees in the first place. Nevertheless, firms have been liable for negligent retention if they failed to remove an employee who showed antisocial traits and later caused harm.

Does this mean that companies can routinely compel a worker to undergo psychological testing as a condition of continued employment? Basically, courts have ruled that it depends on whether an employer has sufficient justification, based on the worker's observed behavior, to require an expert opinion on his or her mental fitness for a particular job. Generally, such justification must be substantial.

For example, a California administrative law judge ruled in 1997 that a college president illegally retaliated against a physical education instructor who filed grievances by requiring him to undergo a psychological evaluation for anger proneness. The ruling was a narrow one, however, and focused on the issue of alleged employer retaliation, not whether the college had the legal right to compel an apparently hot-tempered worker to undergo psychological testing.

Concerning both negligent hiring and negligent retention, it's essential that a contracted firm be qualified to administer and interpret test results. Courts have heard cases of drug tests involving applicants who were not offered employment or employees wrongfully discharged because of the incorrect results of drug tests that were negligently handled. In some of these cases, applicants/employees have successfully sued the employers and drug-testing firms. Similarly, a rejected applicant or fired worker may be successfully able to sue the employer and the consulting firm for negligently conducting and analyzing psychological tests, biodata, and interviews.

3. *What is employee defamation?*   In recent years, a small but significant body of law has severely curtailed the willingness of com-

panies to release information about their former employees. Not long ago, it was routine for companies during the hiring process to obtain detailed descriptions, often in writing or over the phone, from a current or previous employer about an individual's character, including diligence, trustworthiness, and emotional stability. As a result of litigation involving claims of employee defamation, those days are long gone.

At most, companies will now release information only about an individual's work duration and job title (e.g., "Sue Jones worked as a marketing assistant for three years, two months before ending employment at our organization"). In fact, it's precisely because character references have vanished that psychological tests measuring traits like conscientiousness, extraversion, integrity, and leadership have soared in their business usage today.

4. *What is the significance of adverse impact in the use of psychological testing?* Highlighted earlier in this chapter, among the chief possible legal challenges raised against a test is that its usage results in adverse impact, namely, unfair discrimination against certain groups or classes of people, especially those protected by legislation.

For example, it would likely be a violation of law for a company to use a test that leads to significantly lower passing rates for black or Hispanic applicants. For this reason, though certain types of intelligence tests have been scientifically validated for the workplace, these have an adverse impact on protected groups and are, therefore, controversial and often shunned by employers.

5. *How must a psychological test be designed to prevent adverse impact?* Chapter 5 discusses this issue in detail.

6. *What privacy protection do applicants have in the hiring process?* Widespread legislation typically allows employees access to personnel files, the right to correct any erroneous information, and control over its disclosure. At least, such is the law in theory; the reality, of course, is often very different. The Privacy Act of 1974

limits the external disclosure of personnel data of federal employees; state privacy laws also exist, sometimes limiting the dissemination of arrest and conviction data.

7. *Isn't it a violation of the ADA's prohibition of preemployment medical evaluations for companies to administer psychological tests in the hiring process?* The answer is definitely no. Employers are given wide latitude in administering personality instruments, such as assessing the applicant's conscientiousness, extraversion, honesty, explosiveness, or leadership ability, so long as these are not designed to identify a mental impairment or disorder, that is, formulate a psychiatric diagnosis.

    Indeed, it's precisely for this reason that such widely respected clinical instruments as the MMPI-2, the TAT, Draw-a-Person, and the Rorschach inkblot test have virtually disappeared from the hiring process: their usage might well violate the ADA's prohibition of preemployment medical, including psychiatric, evaluations. In this regard, too, the court's ruling in *Soroka v. Dayton Hudson* has undoubtedly had a large impact on eliminating such clinical measures from the workplace.

5

How Tests Are Designed

The field of psychometrics has always been highly specialized, but it has become increasingly so today. Test inventors must not only be knowledgeable about the latest research in personality and motivation, cognition, or educational achievement, as never before, they must also be sensitive to the legal ramifications of their workplace products. As we've seen highlighted in chapter 4, the courts allow a wide leeway in test construction, so long as certain specific psychometric criteria are followed.

Such specialized knowledge doesn't come easily. Well-designed tests these days are worth their proverbial weight in gold, while poorly devised instruments quickly disappear from the business scene. Though few of us will ever be called upon to develop a psychological test aimed at prehires or employees, a basic grasp of assessment is nevertheless helpful. Why? Because whatever our position in today's workplace, we're likely to find such information relevant to our own career advancement.

Elements of Test Design

The field of psychological testing is more than a century old, but its basic features have remained consistent. Whenever a test is constructed, it must meet several specific criteria scientifically, particularly concerning *validity* and *reliability*. The courts have especially emphasized the importance of establishing validity to ensure that a test is nondiscriminatory, that is, free from adverse impact.

First, a test must be proven to be job-related. Not only is this aspect a key to compliance with Equal Employment Opportunity Commission (EEOC) regulations, it also makes eminent sense. There are dozens, if not hundreds, of distinct psychological traits by which we differ from one another. With the advent of computer technology and new, high-powered statistics, it's not hard to measure these. Some are, indeed, quite fascinating, and make for good conversation in parties and dating situations. They also keep many academic researchers busy generating study after study. But in the business world, the question ought certainly be: which of these traits actually relate to job success?

Let's take a concrete example. Psychologists in the food industry know that some of us are definitely chocolate lovers ("chocaholics"), while others dislike the taste. The reason is seen as largely genetic, or at least physiological, rather than primarily due to social factors. And, to be sure, cultural elements are also involved: in many countries, gifts of chocolate and flowers have a romantic connotation. Yet, unless psychologists can prove scientifically that chocolate preference relates to job performance—and, trust me, stranger findings do exist—test questions on this topic are inappropriate.

Let's look at another scenario: pet ownership. We all know people who own three or four cats and lament only that they lack the room at home for more. Others proudly proclaim themselves as ardent dog lovers, and still other folk avoid all contact with both animal species. Is it possible that our liking for cats, dogs, or neither animal is associated with job competence? Yes, it's definitely possible, though not likely. And, if such a link can be demonstrated statistically, then companies can certainly utilize such information in pre-employment and employment assessment.

Know, however, that executives and managers today are essentially interested in six aspects of employee functioning: (1) extraversion, (2) integrity, (3) conscientiousness, (4) stress tolerance, (5) anger control, and (6) leadership. To a growing extent in our new global economy, they are interested in problem-solving style and entrepreneurial ability, respectively. In none of these areas is it necessary for test developers to formulate items that may be afoul of discrimination complaints involving race, gender, ethnicity, or sexual orientation.

After a psychology test has actually been constructed and evaluated experimentally, it must then be standardized on an appropriate sample of the relevant population, and this requires considerable demographic expertise. For example, if a company is developing a preemployment measure of extraversion in the general population, then its sample must accurately reflect the gender, ethnic, and racial composition of the society at large. Otherwise, no matter how scientifically rigorous its design may be in terms of brilliantly worded items with highly relevant job relevance, that test will be rejected as biased according to Civil Rights Act and EEOC guidelines.

Scientific norming is also a process that ensures tests are equivalent across cultures. For instance, all test questions should have the same meaning, regardless of an applicant's ethnic or racial background. Typically, therefore, major American testing firms typically provide translations of their tests into languages besides English, most commonly into Spanish. This is often a difficult task in psychometrics, for the wording of items, as well as their precise meaning, must remain precisely the same to avoid a potential adverse impact.

Validity

Once an accurate sampling takes place for standardization, the next step involves the establishment of *validity*. Four distinct types of validation procedures, or strategies, are currently in vogue. These encompass, respectively:

1. *Construct validity.* Construct validity is the extent to which a test measures a theoretical construct or trait. Examples of such constructs are extraversion, trustworthiness, leadership, and susceptibility to stress. Establishing such validity requires that relevant information is accumulated from a variety of sources.

Any data that shed light on the nature of the trait under consideration and the conditions influencing its development and manifestation are deemed acceptable. Developers of a test being developed to measure trustworthiness, therefore, will look for many workplace examples of either honest or dishonest employee behavior. These may vary widely, from situations of overt theft to those in which workers falsely call in sick, or punch out their friends' time cards.

2. *Content validity*. Content validity basically involves a systematic examination of test content to determine whether it covers a representative sample of the workplace behavior being assessed. Content validity is built into a test from the outset by choosing appropriate items. Such a validation procedure is typically done in evaluating achievement tests, and seems straightforward enough. Thus, a test measuring knowledge of American history or geography should comprise items specifically involving these two subjects, rather than, for example, Russian history or literature.

    When it comes to personality testing, though, this issue truly becomes thorny. For instance, suppose a new test has been created to measure the trait of shyness. Immediately, psychologists start debating the issue of content validity. Does the test really measure shyness, or does it inadvertently measure—at least to an extent—other traits, such as introversion or perhaps even depression? That is, maybe José or Erika is scoring high on this test not because of shyness, but due to a tendency to prefer solitude or because of a depressed outlook.

    In response, the test's defenders might contend: "What do we mean by shyness, anyway? Or introversion? Or even depression? Maybe they're all related in some way that social science doesn't yet fathom." No matter how seemingly definable a personality trait may be, rest assured that as soon as a test is constructed to measure it, that trait will start looking marvelously elusive.

3. *Face validity*. Face validity refers not to the test's validity in the technical sense, but what it superficially appears to measure. It

pertains to whether the test "looks valid" on the face of it. To whom? The people asked to take it, the administrative personnel who decide on its use, and other technically untrained observers.

Face validity is often necessary to ensure the cooperation of both children and adults in psychological testing. It's never a substitute for objectively determined validity, but has an important cosmetic purpose. Much less relevant in personality assessment than in achievement assessment, face validity helps guarantee that individuals will take the test seriously and try their best. And, in our age of noncompliance, this is nothing to sneeze at.

4. *Criterion-related validity.* Criterion-related validity indicates a test's effectiveness in predicting a person's behavior in specified situations. Actually, in the legal sphere discussed in chapter 4, it's the type of validity most respected by courts and governmental agencies involved with employment situations: the relevant weight of legal opinion is that in order for a workplace test to be valid, it must pertain to a meaningful dimension of employee functioning, and such validity concerns criterion-related strategies. Of these, two distinct forms are typically identified: (1) *predictive* and (2) *concurrent* validity.

    With predictive validity, an individual's test score is compared with his or her actual job performance on the particular trait. For instance, an honesty test would be viewed as predictively valid if it differentiated well statistically between new hires found guilty of stealing at work within a specified period of time, for example, one year, versus those who amassed unblemished records.

    Concurrent validity is more commonly used, due to time pressures in industrial research. In this approach, the particular test is administered to a group on whom criterion data are already available. Thus, the scores of existing employees who take an honesty test may be compared with data pertaining to dishonest, or suspected dishonest behavior, found in their personnel files. The courts have taken a very strong position that in undertaking concurrent validity, it's crucial for researchers to look at actual job-related behaviors—in this case, for example, simply comparing honesty test results with supervisors' general ratings of employee productivity would be viewed as inadequately broad.

No matter which type of validation strategy is chosen, it's essential that a relationship be demonstrated between between successful test performance and successful job performance. In one recent case, a preemployment test requiring a sample legal opinion from applicants for a law position was challenged as discriminatory. However, the measure was upheld by the court to be adequately job-related, for it met the requirement of validity.

The issue of what constitutes acceptable test validation is hardly academic, for no hard-and-fast rule can yet be applied by employers interested in avoiding litigation. In addition, there's also a hefty financial factor to consider: the more thorough the validation study, the greater its expense. At some point, every organization must decide whether the cost of a validation effort is worth the potential benefit of psychologically assessing its job applicants or employees.

Reliability

Besides validity, *reliability* is the other key component of all psychological tests. It refers to the consistency of the results, and is typically measured by one of the four following approaches:

1. *Interreliability.* Interreliability is the most obvious, and also the most preferred method. The same person takes the identical test after a specific period of time, and his or her scores are then compared. The test-retest interval is frequently three or six months and only rarely of larger duration. The ideal, of course, is that the individual obtains exactly the same score, or very

close to it. Like all test development techniques, this suffers from several drawbacks: particularly, the influence of "practice" on repeat results on measures of memory, intelligence, academic achievement, or mechanical aptitude.

2. *Alternate-form reliability.* Alternate-form reliability is an approach designed to avoid the problems that are inherent in test-retest reliability. Individuals are presented with alternate forms of the same test over two or more sessions. In this way, they're unbiased by previous exposure to the identical items presented in the identical order.

3. *Split-half reliability.* In psychometric research, this method is frequently used as a way to avoid having to wait up to six months to determine if a test is worthwhile. Individuals are given two comparable halves of the same test, and their scores on the halves are then compared. Because only one test session is involved, the temporal stability of the scores is not examined.

4. *Kuder-Richardson reliability.* This fourth method for finding reliability, named after its two founders, utilizes a single administration of a single form. However, unlike the other methods, it analyzes the consistency of individuals' responses to all items on the test. Mathematically, the Kuder-Richardson reliability score relates to the mean of all split-half coefficients resulting from different splittings of a test.

If test-retest reliability is the preferred method (the others are often dismissively known as *lazy-minded research*), how sensitive nevertheless are personality tests to the changing events we experience in everyday life? Suppose an instrument seeks to measure outgoingness, and the job applicant just had a big, upsetting argument with a best friend the night before? Could it affect her test performance so that, for example, the score becomes lower than would otherwise be the case? Or suppose the job candidate's two-year-old daughter was hospitalized yesterday for asthma. Could that elevate a test score having to do with stress or depression? How about if a job applicant's present company is undergoing massive downsizing, and he's seen virtually his entire department eliminated? Could that influence his score on a test of employee conscientiousness?

Major personality tests do show significant reliability, and in an imperfect world are accepted as worthwhile. But do these tests take such matters into account? The answer is no. I am aware of no instrument that permits the individual to recount a problem or crisis that might be affecting his or her outlook, though an interview might certainly allow it. Intriguingly, though, the courts have proven to be much less concerned about a workplace test's reliability than its validity, perhaps due specifically to the issue of adverse impact.

Adverse Impact: A Closer Look

The EEOC immediately becomes concerned if a test produces different scores among varying subgroups of the American population, such as minorities or women. For example, if documentation reveals that men and women are performing differently on tests of mathematical and verbal ability, these would be subject to legal scrutiny. At the very minimum, a business that used such tests would need to prove that their characteristics were specifically job-related.

Let's examine a hypothetical situation involving dietary preference. Suppose research data show indisputably that clerical workers who consume a lot of meat are more productive than all others. Does this finding automatically allow employers to ask questions of clerical applicants regarding dietary habit, in order to select the heaviest meat eaters? Almost certainly, the answer is no. Why? Because religions like Hinduism, Islam, and Judaism all have major dietary components, and, therefore, such test questions are likely to be seen as discriminatory under Title VII of the Civil Rights Act. Similarly, vegetarians might be able to claim a religious basis for their dietary style and, thus, likewise raise the specter of discrimination.

Let's take a look at another example. Handball, believe it or not, ranks among the favorite participatory sports of some men and women. In New York City, where I grew up during the Cold War, many ethnic neighborhoods boasted handball "stars" who held the status of local celebrities, and even had followings of ardent fans. Suppose psychological research reveals that employees who play handball regularly have less absenteeism than others. Does this allow companies to include test questions about handball activity?

The answer is again no—this time because of the Americans with Disabilities Act. Unquestionably, individuals with a major handicapping condition, such as cerebral palsy, bone disease, severe arthritis, or stroke, would be adversely affected by test questions on handball play, or participation in sports, or even an exercise program in general. Consequently, these items would be considered discriminatory, and regardless of their usefulness in predicting job performance, banned from test inclusion.

In short, it's only half the ball game nowadays for psychometricians to prove that a particular trait, characteristic, or skill validly and reliably predicts employment outcome; while necessary and essential, such proof is not itself sufficient. Rather, test developers must also be sure that items are free from adverse impact.

The Lie Scale

In case you weren't aware of it, people tend to lie. And, believe it or not, men and women are prone to distorting their personal strengths and weaknesses to get hired for a desired job. Whether such employment-related dishonesty is more prevalent now than a generation ago is certainly arguable. Most psychologists would probably say yes and base their opinions on the increased anonymity of American daily life today.

It has recently been estimated that almost a quarter of job candidates lie on their résumés, of whom almost 42 percent are likely to fudge on their educational background or professional affiliations. Significantly, men have been found twice as likely as women to lie on résumés, though why this is so undoubtedly reflects all sorts of social pressures and conditioning. More than ever, employers know that applicant Bob may not have actually graduated from Cornell University, despite what his résumé says, or that Jennifer wasn't really president of her county's real estate association six years ago.

In any event, psychometricians have long known that people inflate their personality traits, and for over a half-century, widely valued tests like the Minnesota Multiphasic Personality Inventory (MMPI) have therefore woven special lie scales into their design. Almost all well-constructed psychology measures today contain these important subscales. Known in the psychometric trade as *softball questions,* these are essentially trick items, included to see if the applicant is trying to fool the tester by pretending to be emotionally more stable, vibrant, and attractive than he or she is in reality.

More than you'd think, this actually happens in the hiring process. If a candidate's score on the lie scale exceeds the predetermined cutoff point, then the test's entire results are considered suspect, and often thrown out. His or her likelihood for getting the position will diminish immediately to near zero. Sometimes, even a couple of lying responses will place a candidate's test results and job application in the human resources department's gray category, rather than its white category for *definitely hire.*

On personality tests, lie items are usually tipped off by questions that contain the words *always, all the time,* or *never.* A few examples here will suffice.

EXAMPLE 1: EVERYTHING I DO IS INTERESTING TO ME.   Note the word *everything.* Nobody on this earth, not even the president of the United States, or your favorite movie star, athlete, or big-name entertainer can legitimately claim this statement to be true. No company expects that every aspect of work—or life, for that matter—will be interesting to employees. Savvy candidates would be wise to moderately disagree with this statement.

EXAMPLE 2: I HAVE NEVER TOLD A LIE.   Note the word *never.* Neither George Washington nor "Honest Abe" Lincoln could validly claim this statement to be accurate. For an applicant to insist that he or she has never lied is obviously absurd. To avoid tripping a resounding alarm on the lie scale, savvy candidates would be better off once more to moderately disagree.

EXAMPLE 3: I HAVE NEVER ACTUALLY LOST MY TEMPER.   The newspapers and magazines today are filled with articles about rage. There's road rage, air rage, and certainly employee rage (known as *going postal*), about which we'll focus later in this book. Workplace violence and sabotage are major concerns nowadays to employers, and they're increasingly turning to personality tests to screen out potential hotheads, misfits, and troublemakers.

But everybody has lost their temper at least occasionally. If a job candidate claims this obvious absurdity, then the lying scale's alarm is definitely going to start resounding. For this reason, applicants who indicate moderate disagreement are making the desired response.

Updating a Test

Finally, no matter how valid or reliable a psychology test is demonstrated to be, its developer must periodically update the norms and relevant statistics in order to satisfy EEOC and ADA guidelines. Likewise, a testing firm that continuously tracks the instrument's possible adverse impact will be viewed more favorably by governmental regulators than one that fails to accomplish such tasks.

Of course, such updating and tracking carries financial costs, as brings administrative headaches as well; for major tests, these burdens can be substantial and involve years of effort. It's definitely among the major reasons why few psychological tests until recently have been revised either in terms of score interpretation or actual content. Particularly for personality measures, though, there has always been ample justification for such updating. For one thing, the English language never remains static, and words and idioms that initially made perfect sense to large numbers of people eventually seem dated and, finally, unfamiliar and even incomprehensible. "Do you often feel blue?" is a clinical item that virtually all adults understood clearly in the 1930s and 1940s; just try presenting the same item to their counterparts today, especially those who hail from other nations.

For another thing, American culture itself—perhaps more than most in the world—seems to change constantly, and corresponding popular attitudes, beliefs, and values do likewise. Not only is this relevant to the issue of "faking" test results among job applicants, but it also means that what was once psychologically abnormal is now mainstream, and equally important, vice versa. For instance, it's likely that American cultural standards regarding workplace honesty and dishonesty have loosened considerably during recent decades. Conversely, the acceptability of sarcastic or joking comments about women or minorities has overwhelmingly tightened.

Personality tests that fail to take language as well as cultural changes into account will, therefore, become increasingly irrelevant and obsolete. Indeed, this process is now happening in the field of applied psychology ever more quickly. Cultural values about personal achievement, success, male-female relations and family life, honesty, stress, self-development, and leadership have altered so much in recent decades that the necessity for up-to-date measures of personality assessment has probably never been greater since their inception nearly a century ago. On legal as well as clinical grounds, updating of even highly valid and reliable tests, therefore, makes eminent sense.

6

Biodata: Would You Hire an Avid Hang Glider?

"Do you wear boxer shorts or briefs?" Former President Bill Clinton was already into his first term of office when the now-famous question was daringly posed to him on MTV. True to character, William Jefferson Clinton smilingly replied, "briefs, but sometimes boxers," and the interviewer turned to seemingly more vital topics. Though few outside the human resources field probably knew it, the question was not only legitimate as a possible indicator of statecraft success, it reflected a well-established means of assessment known as *biodata* (abbreviated from the term *biographical data*).

Indeed, the use of biographical information has long ranked among the most reliable assessment techniques, and is today undergoing an attractive facelift as well. Ironically, respondents' willingness to answer invasive questions about their backgrounds and lifestyles, such as the clothing preference asked of the president of the United States, has been partially responsible for its high utility. For decades attacked by academic psychologists as "scattershot" and lacking roots in personality theory, biodata has nevertheless proven invaluable in differentiating successful workers from those better left unhired. To a much lesser extent, this technique has also played a role in management selection and organizational development.

Reliance upon life history information provided by job applicants rests upon a single, well-known mantra: "The key to future behavior is past behavior." In other words, don't pay inordinate attention to what job applicants tell you about their attitudes, beliefs, and goals. Rather, examine as thoroughly as necessary the actual details of their backgrounds and lifestyles. And the easiest way to do this? By measuring what they write on their application forms. In practice, this outlook hasn't really hindered the use of formal personality testing so much as it has emphasized a multiarrayed approach in employee assessment. And that's surely a good thing.

It was Colonel Thomas L. Peters of the Washington Life Insurance Company of Atlanta, Georgia, who is credited as the inventor of life history analysis for personnel purposes. Back in 1894, he proposed at the Chicago Underwriters' meeting that a way to improve the selection of life insurance agents, a thorny problem in his growing industry, "would be for managers to require all applicants to answer a list of standardized questions, such as the following: Present residence? Residences during the previous ten years? Birth date and place? Marital status? Dependent or not for support on own daily exertions? Amount of unencumbered real estate? Occupation during previous ten years? Previous experience in life insurance selling? For what companies? For what general agents? When and where? Claims, if any, for unsettled accounts? References?"

From today's vantage point, such questions seem obvious enough. But as Peters recounted to an interested audience, his associates in the Georgia Association of Life Insurers had begun using this format with excellent results. Later, during the World War I era, industrial psychologists refined the use of such questionnaires by devising application blanks with personal history sections.

The big breakthrough came in 1922, with psychologist Robert Goldsmith's groundbreaking research. He examined the application forms of 50 highly rated, 50 poorly rated, and 50 middle-rated salespeople from a larger sample of over 500. His goal? To identify the specific aspects of life history that were statistically linked with, and therefore predictive, of employment success.

Goldsmith calculated weighted scores for such diverse factors as age, education, marital status, club membership, previous occupation and previous experience in selling life insurance, whether the candidate her- or himself owned life insurance, and her or his reply to the question, "What amount of insurance are you confident of placing each month?" Some factors had greater predictive power than others. But when the analysis was complete, Goldsmith was able to distinguish effectively among the three categories of salespeople, and he had transformed the conventional application form into what has become known as a *weighted application blank* (WAB).

The underlying principle is familiar to everyone who has owned automobile insurance. Based solely on statistical data—it has never been cost-effective to conduct interviews or administer psychological tests to policy applicants or renewers—insurance companies analyze what sorts of drivers tend to have more accidents and, consequently, charge them higher premiums (e.g., those who have a history of traffic violations or automobile accidents, those who live in certain geographic areas, those who commute long distances to work, or those who drive a sports car).

Posing questions about educational achievement, work history, and family background in an era with minimal governmental regulation of employment practices, the WAB became increasingly used during the 1930s and 1940s in the workplace. Private and public organizations alike found it a valuable hiring tool. For example, an influential study of Chicago department store saleswomen found, based on biographical data, that ideal applicants were well-educated widows between the ages of 35 and 54 who had children and at least five years' previous sales experience—and who, curiously enough, were short and overweight.

Does this mean that a heavier physique among women somehow contributed to their productivity on the sales floor? It's certainly possible, but not necessarily so. The axiom in Statistics 101 is that "correlation does not imply causation." That is, it's just as plausible (and who really knows?) that taller, thinner women opted out of such department store work at a faster rate, for whatever reasons.

It isn't clear precisely when the notion of casting the application blank's item options into a multiple-choice format occurred, but the U.S. military used it to considerable advantage during World War II. The U.S. Army, Navy, and Air Force all utilized multiple-choice life history assessments for screening recruits and training officers. By 1957, the U.S. Army's Adjutant General's Office reported that, after 16 years of research, the biodata blank was the most consistently successful method of predicting peer and tactical officer ratings of leadership. The Adjutant General's Office also noted that a specially constructed inventory key predicted a pass versus resign criterion among officer candidates to a high extent.

Similarly, major research undertaken by the Standard Oil Company of New Jersey several years later found a biographical measure to predict managerial ability accurately. For instance, the most competent executives were those who had been competent in college, pursued leadership opportunities, and saw themselves as forceful, dominant, assertive, and strong.

Some of the specific biodata factors seemed obvious to psychologists familiar with the Standard Oil study: an absence of job hopping, being born locally, being referred by an existing employee, owning a home, being married, belonging to clubs and organizations, and playing sports or physical games. Other factors were decidedly less obvious, such as being raised in a rural or small-town household. And two rather bizarre factors that predicted employee theft were (1) "doesn't want a relative contacted in case of an emergency," and (2) "uses no middle initial." Go figure those out.

Despite definite reliability in an era when personality measures like the Rorschach inkblot test, the MMPI, and the Blacky Test were dominated by Freudian concepts like "oral fixation" and "anal retentiveness" that held minimal job relevance, biodata usage was heavily criticized by academic psychologists. Many were dismayed by its conceptual rootlessness—its nearly total indifference to existing schools of personality theory, whether freudian, adlerian, jungian, or humanistic—and its failure to justify rational grounds for the inclusion of various items.

Thus, Herbert Guion, an influential personality theorist in the 1960s, sneered, "The procedure is raw empiricism in the extreme, the 'score' is the most heterogeneous value imaginable, representing a highly complex and usually unraveled network of information." Another theorist lamented, "It doesn't matter why an item differentiates successful real estate agents from unsuccessful—only that it *does*."

Despite the validity of such criticism, and its value in spurring today what are known as *rationally constructed* (i.e., theoretically based) biodata measures, it's important to know the mantra, "The best predictor of future behavior is past behavior," is hardly restricted only to supporters of biodata measures.

That is, the fields of both educational and clinical psychology have likewise found past performance to be a major indicator of future performance. Statistically, for instance, despite all the professional effort geared to academic aptitude testing, the single best predictor of one's college grade point average is—guess what?—one's high school grade point average. Despite the emergence of well-designed clinical tests like the Beck Depression Scale and the Beck Hopelessness Scale added to such mainstays as the Rorschach inkblot test and the MMPI, the single best predictor of whether a severely depressed man or woman will attempt suicide is whether he or she has tried it previously.

39 SAMPLE BIODATA ITEMS*

1. Marital status.
2. Father's education.
3. Father's occupation.
4. Mother's education.
5. Mother's occupation.
6. One's birth order in family of origin.
7. Size of one's family of origin.
8. One's family happiness while growing up.
9. Relationship with one's parents.
10. How one learned to drive.
11. One's childhood sports activities.
12. Extent of mother's help with choosing one's clothes.
13. Extent of mother's help with one's schoolwork.

---

*Adapted from Stone and Jones, 1997.

14. One's adolescent dating activities.
15. Parental discipline.
16. Family-of-origin income.
17. Family-of-origin economic level.
18. Whether one considered quitting high school.
19. Age at high school graduation.
20. High school interests.
21. Size of high school.
22. High school grade point average.
23. High school standing/rank.
24. How one handled adolescent problems.
25. College size.
26. Time spent studying in college.
27. Job preferences.
28. Executive potential.
29. Speed of work.
30. Extent liked by peers.
31. Extent of club membership.
32. Frequency of leisure activities.
33. Types of leisure activities.
34. Current handling of difficult tasks.
35. Behavior when angry.
36. Driving skills.
37. Headache frequency.
38. Have you ever built a model airplane?
39. Do you repair your own car?

Among the most widely used biodata measures in the United States today is the Initial Career Profile (ICP) System, earlier known as the Aptitude Index Battery (AIB). Especially favored in the insurance industry, it's utilized by many firms for selecting entry-level sales representatives; an estimated tens of thousands of job candidates are annually evaluated with the ICP. Dating back to 1919 in its initial form, the ICP is a composite measure with biographical items that inquire on educational level, employment history, financial status, membership in organizations, and number of dependents, as well as hobbies, personal interests, and personality traits.

Carefully refined over the years, the ICP is designed to measure such qualities as the job applicant's stability-in-work history, commitment to his or her current employment situation, and range of social activities. Organizational psychologists have found such factors to be indicative of one's outlook and approach to both life and work.

How effective actually is the ICP? The results are intriguing. Candidates with low scores clearly make unsuccessful insurance salespeople; they're unlikely to perform well either in terms of career longevity or productivity. But many *high* scorers on the CPS also fail to become successful insurance salespeople. Thus, at least when selecting effective employees in this field, it's necessary that biographical data be buttressed by other measures to maximize predictability; this, in fact, is precisely what major firms in the industry are doing.

Over the years, the U.S. Navy has used a very short WAB, combined with cognitive tests, to select recruits. Among the most salient items of the Navy's WAB are years of schooling completed, expulsions or suspensions from school, age at enlistment, and existence of primary dependents. Based on a huge sample of over 65,000 applicants, Navy psychologists have developed an odds-for-effectiveness statistical table, which allows recruitment staff to read out the "job survival" of an applicant, depending on his or her age, education, cognitive ability, and number of dependents.

Do men and women score similarly on biodata inventories? The general scientific consensus is no. For this reason, the U.S. Navy has utilized different predictors based on gender, as has the Israeli Defense Force. As for the insurance industry's CPS, it can be administered to both men and women, but is scored differently depending on the applicant's gender. Conversely, a biodata inventory used by American Telephone & Telegraph managers has shown equal validity for male and female job candidates. Its developers commented, "The same kinds of experiences and interests that characterize successful managers of one sex are also predictive of success for the other."

Increasingly today, psychologists are seeking to create biodata measures that are better grounded in personality theory, as well as more innovatively designed. Among those active in such work is Dr. Michael Mumford of the American Institute for Research in Washington, D.C., who has aptly noted:

> Students of background data chant an old mantra: "Past behavior is the predictor of future behavior." This statement, however straightforward as it may seem, begs as many questions as it answers. What are the performances I should try to predict with background data? What aspects of a person's life history should be used in our attempts to predict performance? How can I compare and contrast people who have been exposed to qualitatively different environments?

For example, instead of presenting job applicants with traditional items like educational level, membership in clubs or civic organizations, or father's occupation, Dr. Mumford and his colleagues have developed an instrument that also probes the "critical incidents" of their careers, such as how they've handled budgeting and scheduling crises.

Another recent technique is to require job candidates to write an essay concerning such questions as: "Describe an accomplishment at work that you're proud of," "Describe a project that you've found rewarding," or "Describe a situation at work that you found personally stressful."

Legal Considerations

Like personality and cognitive tests, life history instruments must adhere to Equal Employment Opportunity Commission and Americans with Disabilities Act guidelines. Especially in that job applicants seem to find biodata measures as more intrusive and unfair than interviews—and, hence, possibly more likely to trigger litigation—employers have become cautious in formulating items for application forms and biodata instruments. Items that once were nearly indisputably straightforward (e.g., name, address, national origin/

birthplace, military service, and work schedule) now require careful formulation.

For example, it's lawful for an employer to request the applicant's maiden name and previous name if employed under it, but it's illegal to request his or her previous name if it has been legally changed. Likewise, it's lawful to request the location and length of the applicant's current and previous addresses, but it's illegal to inquire about foreign locations including his or her nationality.

As is true for personality tests, if a biodata instrument even inadvertently creates adverse impact, such as pertaining to an ethnic minority, the employer's burden is to prove its job relatedness. Though WABs and biodata inventories typically have excellent predictive validity, their face validity has typically been weak or even nonexistent. Thus, it's likely to prove quite difficult for a company to explain in court why prospective employees whose names lack a middle initial are more likely to steal.

Invasiveness Considerations

Though legal considerations certainly impinge on biodata usage in today's workplace, there's another key reason that many firms have become careful about biodata instruments: applicants often experience these as a violation of privacy. When times are tough economically, many job seekers may decide to "bite the bullet" and answer biographical and lifestyle questions they'd prefer to ignore. In today's unprecedented economic boom, however, prospective employees in many industries know they exert real leverage, and can easily choose a more worker-friendly organization over another.

Currently, this issue is gaining considerable attention in the human resources field; a growing number of professional articles warn that however scientifically valid and legal, certain types of biodata measures are likely to scare away potentially valuable employees. Some applicants may simply walk out the personnel door, while others may turn down an offer because they found the selection process demeaning or offensive.

What kinds of biodata items generally trigger the most dissatisfaction? A recent study found four broad categories aroused the greatest antagonism: (1) those generating fear of stigmatization, (2) worry about having to recall traumatic childhood events, and anxiety about revealing oneself in terms of (3) sexuality and (4) religion. Questions regarding the latter two domains are, of course, illegal. As for the first two categories, professionals would indeed be wise to tread gingerly nowadays to avoid antagonizing job applicants.

Research decisively indicates that an item's face validity is crucial: the more job related it appears even superficially, the more likely applicants are to view it as reasonable. (Whether they'll answer it truthfully is another matter.) For instance, prospective insurance salespeople would be more favorably disposed to an item like, "How long did you stay at your previous job?" than "How many times have you been to a gambling casino in the past five years?"

There's also solid evidence that job applicants resent as intrusive those biodata items probing their childhood and adolescence (e.g., "How many friends did you have in elementary school?" "How often did you date in high school?") or their parents' characteristics, even with such straightforward questions as "mother's occupation" or "father's education." Especially now when many foreign-born workers are in the American labor market, parentally oriented items might well be construed as having adverse impact, such as discriminating against national origin. Why? Because in many economically underdeveloped nations, from El Salvador and Mexico to Pakistan and Senegal, the vast majority of inhabitants lack high school education or white-color job histories.

Interestingly, gender appears to be a significant factor in how people react to potentially invasive questions. The results aren't yet conclusive, and no single psychological explanation has yet convincingly emerged, but questions about childhood, adolescence, current activities and interests, financial status, and employment history are all more likely to antagonize men than women. There's one exception, and that's the question about marital status: women find it a much greater violation of privacy than men. Of course, this question in the employment process is now illegal.

Transportability of Biodata Measures

Just as psychometricians must be sensitive to possible cultural biases and errors in validating personality tests, so, too, for biodata inventories. Generally, research indicates that these don't travel as well as ability tests or even personality tests. Besides the obvious issue of ensuring an accurate translation, there's the far more difficult matter of taking into account different cultural norms and variables. For example, home ownership is much less common in most European, South American, and Asian countries than in the United States and is, therefore, less meaningful as an indicator of financial stability. Likewise, average family size in Mexico or Peru is much higher than in the United States, so this factor may have entirely different predictive validity.

And, while a high school diploma essentially holds the same value in New York, Illinois, or Florida, it has a significantly different status in Pakistan or the Dominican Republic. Likewise, the question, "How many O levels did you pass?" educationally means nothing outside of Britain.

Not only do WABs and biodata measures tend to be culturally specific, they're also specific toward the organization for which they're developed—and toward the criteria against which they were developed. For example, a WAB that predicts a job applicant's ratings by his or her supervisor rarely predicts employment tenure, and vice-versa.

It's mainly for this reason that, despite the success of life history data as an indicator of later job performance, it has seldom been used in managerial selection; traditional biodata prediction models of job performance developed in one context simply do not readily transport into others.

Reliability of Biodata

Finally, though biodata inventories would seem to hold several advantages over the artificiality of personality tests, they're hardly free from the issue of reliability. In particular, academic psychologists today raise two issues about the entire subject of basing hiring, and possibly promotional and training decisions, on the basis of life history information: (1) To what extent can people accurately recall their past experiences and behavior? (2) To what extent *will* people accurately report their past experiences and behavior?

The good news is that research shows that adults are generally capable of giving reliable reports about their past in the workplace. There's also clear evidence, however, that severe distortions and outright errors are rampant when it comes to parents' recollections of their children's early behaviors, traits, and interests. It has also been found that remembrances of our own childhood events are notoriously unreliable, so much so that cognitive researchers are now adopting a whole new conception of memory: that it resembles a continuous mental reconstruction of the past, not a photographic or cinematic recording.

Interestingly, it was the Viennese psychologist Alfred Adler, Freud's long-time nemesis, who argued for precisely this view in the early 1900s based on his therapeutic work. In Adler's viewpoint, however vivid our memories, they're invariably reflections of our *current* adult personality, and not to be viewed as objective truth. So, it's certainly possible that a job applicant's sincere responses about his or her early life are strongly distorted.

How about deliberate falsehoods? The traditional WAB can be faked only if the applicant deliberately lies. Research currently gives conflicting accounts on how often people actually do this in real-life employment situations. Nearly all professionals agree, however, that such fabrication has increased dramatically in recent decades. Most typical embellishments are those overstating one's most recent salary and length of previous employment, as well as those describing part-time positions as full-time employment. Frequently, candidates also deliberately distort why they left their last employment; entirely falsifying a former employer is also common.

Biodata inventories are more like personality tests than are WABs, and can definitely be faked; especially pervasive is the issue of social desirability. In American society, it's consistently been found that people lie on questionnaires and surveys probing such matters as sexual activity, religious worship, physical exercise, voting, and patronage at fast-food restaurants.

For example, if social scientists were naive enough to believe the results of their carefully constructed biodata instruments in marketing and polling research, Americans would be a lot more sexually active, religious, trim, and politically involved than is almost certainly the case in reality. Again, precisely for this reason, data obtained from biodata instruments—with their often obviously "correct" answers—must be integrated with results from other sources including personality tests.

7

What's Your Type?
The Myers-Briggs Type Indicator

Personality study traditionally hasn't been admired much in the business world. Let's face it: most managers and executives have viewed psychology as impractical, even irrelevant, in the quest for profitability; compared with fields like engineering or chemistry, even its fundamental theories have seemed dubious. Generally, few in organizational command have sought more than a smattering of psychological concepts, and often these are only weak simplifications.

It's quite a historical puzzle, therefore, how the Myers-Briggs Type Indicator (MBTI) has come to gain so much popularity in today's workplace. More than 2.5 million men and women annually are administered the Myers-Briggs (as it's popularly known) for purposes ranging from career planning to management and leadership training, and major corporations including Aetna Life and Casualty have been successfully using it for years, too, in the increasingly vital task of team building.

The MBTI originated in the abstruse theory of Swiss psychiatrist Carl Jung, who had initially been close to Sigmund Freud and then broke decisively with him in 1912. Jung regarded Freud as a brilliant but dogmatic thinker, whose overriding emphasis on childhood sexuality was no longer intellectually tenable. Over the next decade,

Jung steadily developed his own approach to personality, which he called analytic psychology. His landmark book, *Psychological Types,* was published in 1921 and translated into English two years later.

The son of a Protestant minister, Jung was deeply interested in such topics as alchemy, mythology, and religious symbolism, all of which he viewed as relevant to understanding our inner world. Throughout his long career, Jung also delved into mysticism and the paranormal, interests that likewise kept his work far from mainstream American psychology. Until well after Jung's death in 1961, his ideas about human nature and growth were obscure to most academic psychologists and counselors.

It's therefore fitting that the MBTI, which has indisputably brought jungian insights to a larger audience globally than any other single test or material, was created neither by professional psychologists nor by therapists. Rather, its inventors were journalist Katharine Briggs and her daughter, novelist-playwright Isabel Myers. Starting in 1923 when Briggs first excitedly read Jung's *Psychological Types* in English translation until Myers' death at the age of 82 in 1980, for more than 50 years the two pioneered successfully as both lay psychologists and women in the technically specialized and male-dominated field of psychometrics.

Interestingly, Jung himself was never directly involved with the MBTI's development. Katherine Briggs corresponded with Jung periodically beginning in 1927, and she arranged to meet him in New York a decade later when he presented his famous Terry lectures at Yale. Joined by Isabel, Katharine told Jung of having loosely formulated a type theory of her own before *Psychological Types* had been published and of having burned her notes after reading this powerful work. Jung replied that she ought not have destroyed her manuscript, as it might have made a real contribution to type psychology. Later, he sent copies of his seminar notes to her.

Nearly 13 years later, in June 1950, Isabel Briggs-Myers was preparing her first trip abroad and wrote to Jung in hopes of meeting with him personally in Zurich. By then, she and her mother had already published several early versions of what was then called the *Briggs-*

Myers Type Indicator. Form A had been copyrighted in 1943, quickly superseded by the more polished Form B; then in 1944, Form C had been completed and immediately begun practical usage as a preemployment test in the banking industry. During the postwar years, an energetic Myers had won growing interest for the MBTI among personnel officials and academic psychologists, including Donald McKinnon, founder of the prestigious Institute for Personality Assessment in Berkeley, California.

"You have no reason to remember me," Myers modestly wrote Jung, "but I met you once in New York before the war at an interview you granted my mother, Katharine C. Briggs." Briefly reviewing that meeting, Isabel then produced a three-page description of the test for which the "psychological insight had been my mother's, the labor and validation of proof has been mine." She enclosed a sample of Form C. What she most wanted to discuss with Jung, Myers confided, "was what *makes* the deficits in type development."

At the time, Jung was unfortunately sick with a flu, and the two would never meet again. But he responded with a gracious letter that praised the Briggs-Myers test and added, "I should say that for any future development of the Type Theory, your Type-Indicator will prove to be of great help."

By the early 1950s, Myers had definitively made the MBTI her life's mission and only semireluctantly put aside her writing career. Her big break came in 1957, when the Educational Testing Service agreed to publish the instrument, which subsequently underwent periodic revisions (updated Forms C through E) during the next few years. In 1975, Consulting Psychologists Press in Palo Alto, California, became the publisher of the MBTI, starting with Form F. A few months before her death in the spring of 1980, Isabel Myers' 82nd birthday was celebrated at the third annual MBTI conference.

Today, the MBTI is most widely used in its 1998 Form M version, encompassing 93 items. Because of its long history and practicality as a research instrument, the MBTI has generated over 400 published studies, including more than 1300 dissertations. The *Journal of Psychological Type* has now published 49 volumes devoted to typological investigations.

The Sixteen-Box Grid

Though Carl Jung's hand was only minimally involved with the MBTI, his theoretical system certainly stands at its center. According to the M-B theory, each of us is born with a predisposition for certain personality preferences. There are four pairs of preference alternatives:

*E*xtraverted	(E)	or	*i*ntroverted	(I)
*S*ensing	(S)	or	i*n*tuitive	(N)
*T*hinking	(T)	or	*f*eeling	(F)
*J*udging	(J)	or	*p*erceiving	(P)

It's important to bear in mind that these eight descriptors reflect preferences; in this regard, jungians offer the analogy of handedness. If you're right handed, it doesn't mean that you never use your left hand, but merely that you prefer the right: you may prefer it strongly or barely at all. The same is true for the other three aforementioned preferences. You may prefer one characteristic a great deal and the other only slightly, or you may decide that you identify with both. Within each pair, though, there is one that you decidedly *prefer*—that you rely upon and to which you more naturally gravitate.

According to the M-B theory, we each develop a preference early in life and remain with it. It would be extremely unlikely, for example, that an extravert will ever become an introvert, or vice versa. As we mature, we rely increasingly on these both intentionally and unintentionally and thereby gain self-confidence and inner strength.

Let's briefly examine these four pairs of preferences. The first dyad is *extravert versus introvert*—undoubtedly, this is the best-known feature of jungian theory, and it's among the first personality traits ever to be identified and measured. They describe the tendency to be either outer-directed or inner-directed in one's emotional focus.

Most people think of extraverts as loud and talkative and introverts as quiet and withdrawn, but these descriptions have much wider significance. In essence, they are polar-opposite qualities that refer to a person's source of energy: what makes him or her feel alive and activated versus sluggish and depleted.

To provide a vivid example: amidst a loud, boisterous party, some individuals quickly become giddy, excited, even exuberant, and find themselves charged up. Others, however, in the exact same setting, soon feel sapped, drained, and even emotionally numb. Within the business world, extraversion has long been linked to effective sales ability and has been viewed with favor. It has also been associated with the tendency to give off clear, easily readable facial expressions. Conversely, introverts have generally been criticized as being bookish and self-absorbed, and offering meager readability of facial expressions and moods.

To avoid falling into a common trap, it's necessary to understand that warmth and likability, what psychometricians now call *agreeableness* (to be discussed in chapter 9), are separate from the extraversion-introversion dimension. There are plenty of extraverts who are cold and friendless (Michigan psychologist Dr. Russ Reeves aptly refers to them as "the car salesperson types with the dead eyes"), and there are many introverts who are empathic and friendly with coworkers. The difference is that the extravert avoids aloneness and seeks out groups, whereas the introvert shuns crowds and prefers relative solitude.

Myers-Briggs consultants estimate that 75 percent of Americans are extraverts, and in sales and public relations positions, the percentage may even be higher. Such persons enjoy participating in meetings and work teams, and generating ideas in the company of others. Introverts are sometimes regarded as shy or aloof, because they seldom initiate or participate actively in meetings, planning sessions, parties, and social occasions. In the workplace, introverts have traditionally been found in relatively solitary jobs like computer programming, accounting, research, and professional writing.

There's little doubt, though, that positions once considered safe for introverts are increasingly viewed as best filled by individuals who can also function well in teams. For this reason, an extraverted accountant, financial analyst, or computer programmer is more likely to be promoted to managerial or executive ranks, if not hired, than his or her introverted counterpart.

The second dyad is *sensor versus intuitive;* this refers to how we gather information about the world. Sensors seek specific answers to specific questions, enjoy practical tasks with tangible results, focus on the present, prefer working with facts and data rather than with imagination, and desire specific instructions. They prefer literalness and sequence. In contrast, intuitives enjoy thought experiments, speculation, and theory building, and they seek generalities rather than specifics. Their preference is for a more figurative, random way of gathering information. It has been estimated that approximately 65 percent of the U.S. population are sensors. In most organizations, there's a decided emphasis on sensors for day-to-day administrative and operations work. Intuitives are seen as often having "their head in the clouds" and being unable to focus well on practical matters.

The third dyad comprises *thinkers versus feelers;* this refers to how we make decisions once we've gathered information. Thinkers pride themselves on their logic, analytic ability, objectivity, and impersonality—believing it's more important to be right than to be liked, and they lend more credence to logic and rationality. Almost all organizational settings favor thinkers for supervisory or managerial positions.

Feelers seek harmony rather than fairness or clarity, tend to overextend themselves to meet others' needs, and consider a "good" decision one that takes others' feelings into account. With a tenderhearted approach to decisions, they prefer subjectivity and interpersonal considerations to the hard facts. Interestingly, research suggests that thinking and feeling are the only two preferences that are gender-related; about two-thirds of men are thinkers and about the same proportion of women are feelers.

The last set of preferences encompasses *judgers versus perceivers;* this pertains to how people prefer to orient their lives. Some M-B theorists view this dyad as the greatest source of workplace tension. Judges prefer decisiveness, planning, punctuality, order, tidiness, organization, adherence to schedules, and control. "A place for everything and everything in its place" is their motto. Conversely, perceivers prefer flexibility, spontaneity, and adaptiveness, and they abhor structure and routine. Generally, judgers are more likely to be found in hierarchical settings such as governmental agencies and large corporations; perceivers are more comfortable in setting their own hours with minimal rules, and are often self-employed or entrepreneurial.

To those familiar with the MBTI, the foremost consideration in assessing an employee is his or her type, comprising 4 traits in sequence, of the 16 possibilities. This sequence becomes a psychological shorthand for understanding each person's basic nature and manner of functioning in a variety of situations and settings. Thus, if I tell you that I'm an INTP but my business partner is an ESFJ, that conveys a tremendous amount of information to those who are well versed in this system. The M-B system also includes the notion of subordinate, auxiliary functions in our personality makeup and resulting behavior, but their role is decidedly less significant in our everyday lives.

Recently, M-B theorists have strongly emphasized the four temperaments that emerge from this system: that is, two-letter combinations. The first letter of a temperament is either S or N; the second letter is determined by the first letter. For instance, intuitives prefer to gather information abstractly and conceptually, and their second most important preference is how they evaluate the data they've gathered: objectively (thinking) or subjectively (feeling). For intuitives, then, the two basic temperaments are NF and NT.

NFs represent about 12 percent of the U.S. population and see the world's possibilities. They tend to be idealists who serve causes that advance humanity's interests: teaching, counseling, humanities, religion, and family medicine. With a positive, idealistic bent, NFs often have difficulty being supervisors and tend to give employees too much leeway. They tend to personalize work issues, and their feelings are easily hurt. For them, the most important thing is for the workplace to be harmonious.

NTs also represent about 12 percent of the U.S. population, and their driving force is to intellectualize everything. They maintain their own standards and benchmarks for what's competent, and they relentlessly pursue excellence. They're frequently perceived by others as aloof, intellectual snobs. In work settings, NTs tend to be strategic planners and researchers, but they can get lost in the strategies and overlook day-to-day business.

If you're a sensor, your preference for gathering information is concrete and tactile. The second most important preference isn't how you evaluate the data, but what you do with them: do you organize them (judging) or continue to take them in, perhaps even seeking more (perceiving?) Therefore, for sensors, the two temperament groups are SJ and SP.

SJs seek to belong to meaningful institutions. Practical and realistic, they comprise approximately 38 percent of the U.S. population, and thrive by procedure and organization. Their strengths are administration, dependability, the ability to take charge, and respecting organizational hierarchies.

SPs focus on immediate problem solving and tasks. Their quest is for action, and they prefer hands-on activities, practicality, and resourcefulness. Comprising approximately 38 percent of the U.S. population, they're attracted to careers that have immediate, tangible rewards: fire fighting, emergency medicine, mechanics, agronomy, building construction and maintenance, carpentry, and anything involving technical skills.

According to M-B theory, how do people change emotionally and grow? Personality maturation is seen to depend on gaining competence with preferred functions, strengthening less preferred functions, and achieving function synthesis and flexibility.

Applying the Myers-Briggs

What does all this mean in practical terms? In recent years, organizational consultants have used the MBTI in such areas as time management, goal setting, team building, problem solving, stress management, leadership training, and conflict resolution.

One of the major uses of the MBTI to emerge has been in career planning. While traditional vocational measures like the Strong Vocational Interest Blank and, more recently, the Self-Directed Search (SDS), developed by Dr. John Holland, have sought to link specific careers like teaching, sales, or scientific research to job-related interests, the MBTI offers a broader agenda. Career counselor Elena Estrin at New York City's Globe Institute of Technology has observed, "Our students take the Myers-Briggs when deciding to change a career, or starting the interview process, or when they simply want to learn more about their job preferences, strengths, and weaknesses. Many are fascinated by the results. The test is also useful for counseling people who are already working and dissatisfied with what they're doing."

Estrin cites the example of an office manager in a law firm who had been an unsuccessful, aspiring actress for several years. "Her test results showed nothing that related to artistic tendencies like Intuition and Feeling. Instead, she scored as a very practical, detail-oriented Sensing and Judging person, who was, in fact, well-suited to administrative work. When we talked more, it became clear that her real problem wasn't her job, but her rocky marriage to a successful artist who had a very different Myers-Briggs type. She had been trying to emulate him by deciding she was really a misplaced actress, and that wasn't who she was at all."

Reflecting New York City's multiethnic composition, Russian-born Estrin also finds the MBTI useful for training foreign students in the interview process.

> There's no doubt that Russians are more introverted than Americans, and from my own experience, much higher on Feeling, Intuition, and perhaps also Perception. People coming from less extraverted cultures, like many Asians, have to learn how to adapt to the expectations of interviewers, or they'll come across as aloof and uninvolved. In the United States, if you don't look into an interviewer or supervisor's eyes when you speak, it's a sign you're lying or evasive. But among Chinese, Japanese, and Russians, it shows respect. For those coming to work in the United States, it's often necessary to be trained in extraversion, such as speaking in a more animated way, making good eye contact, or giving a firm handshake, in order to make the best impression.

In this light, a recent study involving the MBTI focused on hospice volunteers, the majority of whom were male college graduates. They tended to be more prevalent in extraversion, intuition, and feeling than the general population; indeed, 75 percent were extraverts and more than 75 percent were feelers. Evidence pointed to the sensing-versus-intuition dyad as the most related to occupational choice: the most common type among volunteers was the INFP, and also prevalent were ISTJs, ISTPs, and ISFJs. As the researchers noted, ISTs are typically described as thoughtful realists who prefer dealing with the "hard facts" of situations in an impersonal manner, and thus display a very practical, matter-of-fact approach when coping with the world. Their introversion and thinking dimensions result in a personality that's the most removed from daily social interaction, and slowest to develop social skills.

The MBTI also has implications regarding employee wellness and absenteeism. A study of adults with coronary heart disease showed they were disproportionately sensing and feeling (i.e., SF in their pair, and especially sensing types). Such persons tend to focus on immediate experience and develop characteristics such as realism, memory for details, and practicality. They also have a strong need for order and are steady workers who may become impatient when details become too complicated. Sensing types dislike new problems unless there are standard ways to solve them.

In contrast, persons oriented to the use of the feeling preference have an understanding of people, a need for affiliation, a capacity for warmth, and a desire for harmony. Research suggests that such characteristics seem to act as a buffer against the development of coronary heart disease, and perhaps other chronic illnesses as well.

Psychological consultant Dr. Russ Reeves in the Detroit area has been applying the MBTI for more than a decade in executive coaching. "It's based on my assumption that instead of trying to change people, you find out who they are and then play to their strengths. With the MBTI, you discover how to play to your good side." Dr. Reeves has found that one of its chief advantages is the nonintrusiveness of test items, an aspect that makes managers and executives much more likely to view their personality results seriously: "You're not asking people about sex, or their toilet-training, or if they would rather eat porridge or drink a martini before killing their mother. You've got a very powerful, non-intrusive test that provides a huge amount of information."

As an assessment tool for team building, Dr. Reeves also finds the MBTI effective. "If you're in an organization with a modicum of trust, you request all the executives to take the test and encourage them to share their results with everyone else. It helps people to understand who they're dealing with in a non-judgmental way. So Larry realizes that he's a Judger and Karen's a Perceiver, and that's why they constantly disagree about the necessity for scheduling meetings and setting deadlines. It's not because Karen is trying to give him a hard time.

"You can also build synergy in work-teams by understanding type and how they differ. For instance, if you pair an Introvert Judging person with an Extrovert Perceiver, you avoid cloning each person's strengths and weaknesses. In this way, the detail-oriented person can be matched successfully with someone who focuses on the big picture. Not only can people play to each others' strengths in that way, they can also cover each others' backs."

The MBTI is not without criticism, of course. For one thing, even many researchers who advocate its usage are disturbed by its "either-or" categorization of major personality traits. Yes, they argue, people can be meaningfully identified with regard to extraversion-introversion. Is it reasonable to assert, though, as does the MBTI, that each of us is *either* an introvert or extravert, thinker or feeler, sensor or intuitor, judger or perceiver? Especially in that the MBTI offers a range of possible scores on each of the four scales, such a dichotomous approach seems unwarranted. Certainly, it seems reasonable to suggest that a very mild introvert and a very mild extravert may behave more similarly at meetings than an extreme introvert and a very mild introvert. Yet, the MBTI provides no vehicle in its scoring even to investigate this possibility: we're an introvert or not.

In this regard, the MBTI's classic comparison of the four dichotomies to the physical dichotomy of handedness just doesn't seem tenable. Rather, personality traits such as extraversion seem more likely to exist on a nondichotomous range, similar to physio-psychological qualities like activity level and degree of moodiness. That is, we're not *either* highly active or a couch potato, and we're not *either* moody or complacent; each of us manifests such vital aspects of temperament on a continuum.

Another criticism pertains to the job relatedness of the MBTI. Although many organizations have undoubtedly found it useful in helping managers and executives to understand themselves better, it's still unclear whether such knowledge produces tangible financial or administrative benefit—and how long such benefit actually lasts. The discouraging statistics on marriage counseling show that even highly motivated men and women find it arduous, over months of sessions, to change their habitual behavioral patterns, such as handling conflicts. Is a half-day or even a two-day management seminar based on the MBTI likely to prove more effective?

Similarly, organizational theorists like Kathy Kolbe, whose work on problem-solving styles we'll examine in chapter 10, question whether the MBTI's four dimensions are relevant to the workplace with its fundamental emphasis on performing tasks. From her perspective, "The Myers-Briggs may be wonderful in showing why two co-workers, both of whom are, say, feeling-introverts like to socialize together on weekends, or will become friends, but what does this really have to do with productivity? More important on the job is to determine how people solve real problems and get things done—and that's a different dimension of the mind."

Yet another criticism of the MBTI relates more to its training application than to its theoretical relevance. That is, some observers argue that MBTI trainers all too frequently in management and leadership seminars extol certain of the 16 types such as the ENTJ, and belittle others like the INFP—reflecting, of course, their own personality biases. Licensed clinical psychologists such as Dr. Naomi Quenk, author of *Essentials of Myers-Briggs Type Indicator Assessment,* may emphasize, "All 16 types are . . . valid and legitimate ways of being psychologically healthy, adapted, and successful," but many MBTI consultants are less credentialed, and show definite biases regarding specific types that may wreak more damage than support among employees.

Despite the validity of such criticism, there's little doubt that the MBTI will have organizational appeal in the forseeable future. In offering both a coherent theoretical system for understanding personality and a noninvasive, easily scored measure with thousands of corroborative studies, its continuing relevance seems well assured.

In this light, a fascinating indicator comes from the contemporary high-tech world. Communications specialist Dr. Clifford Nash at Stanford University has undertaken a series of studies with wide applicability for e-commerce, such as website design and online sales and auctions. Specifically, Dr. Nash has found that computerized voices are identifiable as either extraverted or introverted, depending on their pitch variability—and, as measured by the MBTI, extraverts are more attracted to computerized voices that are extraverted, whereas introverts prefer those similar to their own monotone style.

Will engineers soon be designing computers, websites, and programs to appeal not merely to extraverts or introverts, but to each of the 16 MBTI types? It appears quite possible, and who knows what other applications lie in store? Clearly, Jung's nearly century-old personality system, psychometrically developed by Briggs and Myers, will exert considerable impact in coming years.

8

Stroking Diogenes:
The Search for Integrity

We all have definite opinions about character, and the goal of determining it accurately has become a national quest. So at the outset, here's an important question: Among all your acquaintances, whom do you most admire for their integrity? And on what do you base your opinion? Could you be totally wrong? Is *anyone* truly honest or trustworthy?

Dating at least as far back as Diogenes, who mockingly carried a lantern in Athens daylight to find such a person, philosophers have debated this question. Are people who seem truthful and upright really so, or just putting on a good show? How can we tell the difference? In an increasingly impersonal society, where few of us even know our next-door neighbor well, let alone the job candidate sitting impassively before us, the issue is hardly just philosophical.

Employee theft is a huge and multi-billion-dollar problem in the American workplace. For anyone with an idealistic bent, the statistics are dismaying. Experts estimate that such thievery is 10 times more costly than street crime, and is responsible for 30 to 50 percent of all business failures. Organizational losses due to employee theft are estimated at $23 billion annually. The dollar amount per incident is close to nine times that involving customer shoplifting. In 1999, 1 of 24 employees was apprehended for stealing—an increase of 11 percent in one year and almost 25 percent in merely two years.

To almost all security consultants, such numbers represent the tip of the proverbial iceberg: for each worker who actually gets caught, there are probably six more eluding detection. Studies suggest that over 75 percent of all individuals have stolen on the job at least once, and that many engage in theft as a regular part of their workplace behavior.

If you believe that it's a problem restricted to entry-level sales clerks filching jeans or sneakers, think again—it pervades all employment ranks. A recent issue of *Security* reported that the average loss from check fraud by employees was $624,000 in 1998, twice the amount a similar survey found four years earlier. Losses due to employee usage of company ATM cards also doubled to an average of $300,000. Security incidents relating to company credit cards tripled over the same period to an average loss of $1.1 million.

Indeed, the greatest rise in employee theft involved travel and expense fraud, hardly the domain of hourly salespeople, increasing seven times over four years to an average of $141,000 in 1998. While many security systems target bookkeepers, loading-dock workers, and mailroom staff as the key perpetrators, research reveals that the greatest losses due to employee theft involve high-ranking managers and executives. It's well known in the corporate world that some of the largest incidents of embezzlement, increasingly involving computerized transfers of funds, are never made public at all.

Though average citizens may not fully grasp the magnitude of employee theft, organizational leaders are well aware of the staggering costs—with no end in sight. Whether workers today are truly more likely to engage in thievery involving money, supplies, equipment, and paid time than in the past is an unresolved question among human resource professionals. The consensus seems to be yes, worker honesty has diminished during the past generation, because organizational loyalty has largely disappeared in an era of massive layoffs, unprecedented downsizing, and reengineering at all levels. It's a trend that is unrestricted to the United States; even in seemingly unchanging countries, such as Japan, where lifetime employment has been almost guaranteed in exchange for unstinting worker loyalty to the enterprise, the equation is quickly altering.

As might be expected in this behavioral climate, the screening of potentially dishonest employees has become a booming business. Mainly known as *integrity testing*, it's a specialty that has soared in managerial popularity since Congress enacted the Polygraph Protection Act in 1988, banning lie detectors from most of the private sector. Each year, millions of men and women are now required to take integrity tests, especially in applying for lower-level sales or banking positions. Whether administered directly online via the Internet or in paper-and-pencil format, the tests generate almost instantaneous information about the trustworthiness of candidates.

Unfortunately, exact data about the usage of integrity assessment are notoriously difficult for outside researchers to obtain. Publishers have consistently been secretive about releasing scientific, as well as business, details concerning these tests and, for example, have strongly resisted the American Psychological Association's (APA's) efforts several years ago to gather accurate information on this field. Many firms flatly refused to provide any statistical data on the standardization method and reliability of their measures, such as their percentage of false positives (i.e., how often they falsely indicated honest test takers to be unworthy of being hired). In this sense, integrity tests are murkier than most widely used psychological instruments like the Myers-Briggs Type Indicator or the Minnesota Multiphasic Personality Inventory—II, which generate hundreds of independent studies by graduate students and academicians around the globe and yield vigorous discussion.

Why all the secrecy? For one thing, publishers claim that releasing detailed information about integrity tests might allow job applicants to better cheat on them. It's unlikely, however, that candidates for such positions as security guard or salesclerk would be reading technical psychology journals. More probable is the explanation that the testing-and-consulting industry is fiercely competitive, and companies view their products and services as highly proprietary. Executives are undoubtedly more worried about how their competitors will take advantage of information on specific test design, validation, and application than they are about job candidates' access to such matters.

Another important explanation lies in the origins of integrity testing. As psychometrician Dr. John Miner cogently pointed out in his
book *Honesty Testing*, measures of employee honesty have generally
emerged not from academic or clinical psychology, but from the
security industry, particularly after polygraph testing was barraged by
public criticism. Thus, for example, the Stanton Survey, a widely
used integrity test, is published by the Pinkerton Services Group, a
longtime corporate security firm. In the corporate security industry,
more than most in the private sector, a willingness to disclose—
much less openly debate—technical information on one's products
or services is virtually nonexistent.

In 1990, the Office of Technology Assessment (OTA) of the U.S.
Congress investigated the use of integrity tests to help determine
what legislative action, if any, was warranted. Guided by the same
concern for employee privacy and dignity that had led to its harsh
criticism of polygraph testing, OTA researchers focused on public
policy issues, such as potential errors in selection decisions, the
effect these tests have on labeling job applicants, and individuals'
reduced employment opportunities.

In its report, the OTA strongly criticized integrity assessment and
claimed that test reliability was poor. By judging employee theft as 3
percent of the workforce, a statistic grossly lower than the 28 to 62
percent estimated by earlier investigators, the OTA asserted that
integrity measures produced an unacceptably high number of false
positives. The OTA, however, stopped short of actually recommend-
ing that Congress ban the tests.

At the same time, the APA launched its own study, with a different
agenda. Written by psychologists for other psychologists and test
users, its direct focus wasn't on policy making but on scientific and
technical issues: How did integrity tests define dishonesty as a theoretical construct, identify appropriate criteria, and establish adequate
validity and reliability? How were test results scored and interpreted?
It's important to note that the APA did not evaluate the tests against
an absolute level of validity; rather, it evaluated them comparatively
(i.e., against other ways to measure job applicants' honesty).

Conceding the reality of significant employee theft today, APA researchers observed that the main alternatives to integrity tests were either structured or unstructured preemployment interviews, extensive background checks, or surveillance efforts. All had their own methodological and financial drawbacks.

Structured interviews were scientifically well validated, but essentially probed the same topics as did integrity measures in a more costly and time-consuming way. Unstructured interviews had minimal predictive validity regarding employee honesty, and detailed background checks and surveillance methods were prohibitively expensive for hiring large numbers of entry-level workers with their typically high job turnover rates. The APA also recognized that recent research revealed that job applicants regarded lie detectors, drug tests, medical examinations, and background checks as more invasive and demeaning than written integrity tests.

Both the OTA and the APA essentially agreed in the early 1990s that integrity testing was certainly preferable in the workplace to polygraphs, but that integrity publishers and consultants needed to better meet ethical and scientific standards, lest these tests eventually produce public outcry and legislative prohibition.

Among leading psychometricians such as Dr. Miner, there's general consensus that the integrity-testing industry is highly concentrated, and that as few as three publishers possess at least half of the total market. While an estimated 50 different tests are generally available, often in several versions, these repeatedly share conceptual and methodological commonalties.

In this entire field, the most important distinction is whether an integrity test is *overt* (i.e., directly probing applicants' attitudes and behavior involving theft and counterproductivity) or *covert* (i.e., personality based and assessing such broad traits as conscientiousness or affability, which psychologists conceptualize as predicting on-the-job honesty).

Designed mainly by security industry experts, overt integrity measures reflect their origins in polygraph testing. As such, their purpose is straightforward: to minimize the prevalence and magnitude of employee theft and related forms of dishonesty. Respondents are directly asked for their opinions regarding objectionable and/or illegal behavior (e.g., "Do you think laws against shoplifting are too harsh?") and their reactions to hypothetical situations involving such conduct (e.g., "Would you always tell your supervisor if you saw a coworker stealing merchandise?"). Questions are typically posed in either a *yes*-or-*no* or Likert scale format. The sole focus of such measures is the individual's degree of honesty, and there's no larger exploration of his or her personality strengths, weaknesses, skills, and interests.

Among the most widely used overt integrity tests is the Personnel Selection Inventory (PSI), published in more than a dozen versions by London House. One of the few such measures to have been subjected to significant independent research, the PSI is targeted at entry-level and midlevel employees. Encompassing 20 subscales on job-related attitudes and behaviors, the PSI is perhaps best known for its honesty scale, which specifically identifies the likelihood that the candidate will not steal cash and merchandise from work. In addition to reporting an applicant's individual scaled score, PSI reports include a list of significant behavioral indicators that help pinpoint potential "danger areas," such as irritability or unwillingness to accept criticism from supervisors.

The PS1-7RST is a covert instrument that encompasses the dimensions of honesty, responsibility, drug avoidance, customer relations, safety, work values, and supervision attitudes, with additional validity and accuracy subscales. As part of the PSI-3, the honesty scale has been found to accurately predict theft admissions made in preemployment polygraph examinations, as well as supervisors' ratings of employee dishonesty, and applicants who are likely to get caught stealing once hired, who have a criminal history of armed robbery and similar offenses, or who are likely to make theft admissions in an anonymous testing situation.

A second major overt integrity test is the Reid Report, published by Reid Psychological Systems, and likewise used predominantly in preemployment screening. Developed by Herbert Reid in 1951, it's among the oldest of such instruments and has been revised over the years. Similar to the PSI, the Reid Report exists in a variety of versions, involving combinations of different scales, and it is aimed mainly at entry-level and midlevel candidates.

Currently, the most widely used version appears to be the Abbreviated Reid Report, a multipurpose measure identifying a potential employee's attitudes related to honesty, conscientiousness, substance abuse, and personal achievement. Based on the responses, the employer receives a printed profile and for each subtest score, one of six possible grades: (1) recommended, (2) qualified recommended, (3) recommended, (4) low risk, (5) high risk, and (6) not recommended.

To its professional credit, Reid Psychological Systems issues periodic research studies. Not surprisingly, these affirm that the Reid Report is highly effective in reducing employee theft at retail drug stores, convenience stores, and similar settings in the United States and Canada. Interestingly, data from the Reid Psychological System's own studies suggest that 20 percent of job applicants in some instances are inaccurately eliminated from hiring due to their responses.

Recognizing that such a false positive rate seems rather high, Reid's researchers nevertheless contended, "The Discharge for Theft criterion undoubtedly underestimates actual theft, since so many do not get caught . . . It is clear that *among those hired,* the Reid Report significantly reduces the incidence of those who turn out later to be dishonest."

The Stanton Survey, mentioned earlier in this chapter, is a third major overt integrity test. Originally published in 1964 and last revised in 1995, it also ranks among the oldest of such instruments. The Stanton Survey comprises 83 questions; most are in a *yes*-or-*no* format, though some are posed on a four-point Likert scale. The test also includes a biodata section with questions focusing on educational background and employment history.

According to several published reports, these three instruments— the PSI, the Reid Report, and the Stanton Survey—comprise fully 50 percent of the overt integrity-testing market. Research indicates that these three measures correlate highly with each other, and that they all tap into a higher-order construct of integrity, assessing conscientiousness, agreeableness, and emotional stability in that order.

Another major instrument is the PSC Survey ADT, a preemployment screening test that provides scores on three scales: (1) trustworthiness, (2) alienation, and (3) drinking and drugs. In its abbreviated form, the test comprises 100 items to which the job applicant chooses either a *yes, no,* or *cannot say*(?) response option. The trustworthiness scale is the largest of the scales, consisting of items probing attitudes toward theft, honesty, and trustworthy behavior on the job. The alienation scale measures attitudes toward rules and regulations, company policies, and respect for supervisors and other authority figures. As its name implies, the drinking-and-drugs scale assesses attitudes toward alcohol and drug use.

The main premise underlying all such tests is that dishonest individuals will view such behaviors and situations differently than their honest counterparts. Over and over again, research has revealed that people most likely to steal are those who have a cynical, dog-eat-dog philosophy of life. Relatedly, applicants who endorse the view that "everyone steals occasionally" or "it's human nature to steal" or "nobody is truly honest" are those most likely to engage in workplace theft.

In this context, it's useful to note that psychological tests are sometimes more complicated than necessary. Among clinical psychologists, a story, perhaps apocryphal, has long circulated in this regard: During the height of the Cold War, the U.S. Air Force needed to psychologically screen service personnel for missile-tracking radar work in Alaska involving long assignments. Though an extensive battery of personality questions was administered, the best statistical predictor of who would complete the Alaskan assignment comprised a single question: "Do you like cold weather?" Similarly, psychologists today find that a single integrity question has immense predictive utility: "Do you believe that people are basically honest?"

In this entire discussion, it's useful to look at a sample overt integrity test. I have created items that present the broad gamut of typical questions; respondents are often required to answer either *true* or *false*.

A SAMPLE OVERT INTEGRITY TEST

1. Most people are honest by nature.
2. If given the chance, most people would not steal a small item from a store if they knew they would never get caught.
3. Nearly everyone has shoplifted as a child or teenager.
4. Most people can be trusted.
5. I would be tempted to steal something I really wanted at work.
6. Parents should be very concerned about a child who steals from classmates.
7. Most youngsters do not steal from friends or classmates.
8. A lot of the teenagers I knew in high school shoplifted at least occasionally.
9. Parents should definitely make a fuss about a teenager who is caught shoplifting.
10. It's really not a primary duty of parents to teach their kids to be honest.
11. I sometimes think about robbing a bank or jewelry store and getting away with it.
12. It can't be considered human nature to steal from others.
13. I have often been tempted to steal things at work.
14. If I knew I would never get caught, I would have no guilt about taking a nice new coat I saw unattended in a store.
15. I believe that our society's laws against shoplifting are way too harsh.
16. If someone finds a wallet or purse in a store, it's wrong to take out any cash before handing it over to the manager.
17. I wouldn't report a coworker I saw stealing merchandise, because it's none of my business.
18. Employees who leave work early without permission are not really stealing from their company.
19. It's wrong to call in sick occasionally to take a day off for rest and relaxation.

20. Employees who call in sick frequently probably just need the rest.
21. An employee who sees a coworker taking supplies home should always report it to his or her supervisor.
22. An employee who occasionally takes supplies home is not really stealing.
23. I have friends at work who steal merchandise occasionally.
24. An employee who is caught taking minor supplies home should definitely not be fired.
25. If someone is undercharged in a restaurant, he or she should not tell the waiter or waitress.
26. It is wrong to buy merchandise that you know is stolen.
27. If an employee accidentally receives too much money in a paycheck, it's a form of stealing not to report it.
28. A company should hire a person who was fired from his or her last job for stealing.
29. If I found a bag of money on the street, I would seriously think about keeping it.
30. I know a lot of dishonest people.

What was your reaction to this sample test? I've found that nonpsychologists typically have two negative reactions: (1) The questions are unfair because everything in life is ambiguous; and (2) the correct answers are so obvious that such tests can't really be dependable predictors. Both criticisms certainly seem valid on their face, so let's examine them critically. Remember, this isn't just a philosophical subject; annually, billions of dollars are involved and are at stake in employee theft.

Criticism No. 1: The questions are unfair because they force black-and-white judgments in a world of grey and ambiguity.

This means that many observers may rightfully protest that "I've never shoplifted in my life, yet I certainly believe that most people are dishonest! Does that mean I wouldn't be hired for a retail sales job?" Unfortunately, the answer may be yes.

The key issue is that decision making in the business world is geared to probabilities: the likelihood of a Boeing 747 making 10,000 flights safely before it's unsafe to travel anymore, or of an automobile tire blowing out before 30,000 miles. In a world of habitual shoplifters and career criminals, many employers are justifiably worried about the damage a new hire can inflict.

As a result, they'd much rather have a few false positives (i.e., honest candidates who are erroneously rejected as dishonest due to their responses) than allow a theft-minded candidate to join the organization. And, as mentioned earlier, data consistently show that individuals with a cynical, dog-eat-dog outlook are the most likely to steal on the job.

Criticism No. 2: The correct answers are so obvious that nobody would be foolish enough to give the wrong reply.

Among the most frequently voiced objections to overt integrity measures is that the correct or socially desirable responses are so obvious that "only an idiot would answer the wrong way." Not surprisingly, the issue of fakability isn't one that test developers often like to address. Nevertheless, research consistently shows that faking is only a minimal problem for overt integrity tests.

For example, a recently published study by Hayes International analyzed the responses of 20,000 retail job applicants, randomly selected, who had taken integrity tests during 1999 and confirmed that they were remarkably self-revealing about their dishonesty. Overall, 22.6 percent scored as high risk due to their answers. Particularly intriguing were their admissions:

- 28.7 percent said they could be tempted to steal from their employer.
- 21.8 percent reported they had frequently associated in the past with fellow employees who admitted to stealing from their employer.
- 18.3 percent said they had stolen money in the past three years.
- 14.5 percent admitted to stealing merchandise in the past three years.

- 12.7 percent acknowledged that they were not honest and might steal or cheat.

As highlighted in chapter 6, research indicates that people are more likely to reveal their attitudes and values than their misconduct or personal behavior in general. This fact is well known to sexologists, who find that people are notoriously unreliable when questioned on their frequency and type of sexual behavior. The false reporting problem also dominates inquiries on religious activity, such as frequency of worship; people's answers are skewed in favor of perceived social desirability or correctness. Many social scientists believe the same problem dogs research assessing ethnic, racial, and religious prejudice, or even voting likelihood.

Thus, questions such as "Do you believe that most people have shoplifted?" are more likely to elicit an honest answer than the direct "Have you ever shoplifted?" or "How often have you stolen something at work in the past three years?" In a nutshell, when questions probe attitudes and values, most job applicants respond truthfully. It should be recognized, however, that research also shows that people are capable of distorting their true responses on integrity tests if encouraged to do so. Indeed, a recent study that male inmates in a medium-security Alabama state prison were able to bolster their honesty scores on the PSC Survey ADT when told to respond in such a way as to make the most favorable impression possible.

In recent years, both covert and personality-based integrity measures have relied increasingly on a lie scale or a validity scale to determine if applicants are trying to fool the tester by pretending to be more trustworthy, reliable, or stable than they really are. Such scales typically include items like, "I have never told a lie" or "I have never lost my temper," which are impossible for all but saints to affirm as true.

Typically, if the applicant scores above the cutoff point on the lie or validity scale, his or her entire test results are considered suspect, and the likelihood of being recommended for hiring diminishes to near zero. Yet, in a U.S. economy today in which the true unemployment is close to zero in many communities, companies are willing to hire candidates whose scores on overt integrity tests—and on lie or validity scales—have previously been considered unacceptably high and risky.

Covert instruments are also used frequently in screening employee honesty. Also known as *personality-oriented* and *veiled-* or *disguised-purpose tests,* these utilize items that generally are commonly employed in personality measurement. They're intended to measure characteristics related to honesty broadly defined, such as thrill-seeking, hostility toward authority, anger proneness, and unreliability. Self-report items might include, "I like to watch speed racing," "I often daydream on the job," and "I can get really mad if someone criticizes my work."

Rather than emerging from the security industry with its polygraph orientation, such measures have generally been created by academic psychologists. The most widely used tests include the Personnel Reaction Blank, the PDI Employment Inventory, the reliability scale of the Hogan Personnel Selection Series, the responsibility scale of the California Personality Inventory, and the Employee Reliability Inventory.

The following questionnaire provides a sample of representative items.

A SAMPLE PERSONALITY-ORIENTED INTEGRITY TEST

1. I love the feeling of a job well done.
2. In my opinion, a job that isn't done perfectly isn't really done.
3. The most successful people are those who always complete what they begin.
4. It's unreasonable to think that every job can be completed on time.
5. Sometimes, it's okay to leave a job unfinished if you know that a coworker will end up finishing it well.
6. I have never forgotten to show up for an appointment.
7. Employees should generally be expected to work extra hours to finish a job on time.

8. I know many people who work themselves too hard.
9. I admire people who put in long hours at work.
10. I am never messy in my work habits.
11. People who know me sometimes say I work too hard.
12. It's important for me to feel productive at work.
13. Being organized at work is not always necessary.
14. I feel sorry for people who put in long hours at work.
15. People who know me often call me a "team player."
16. Being part of a team is basic to most jobs today.
17. I would avoid hiring someone who didn't seem to be a "team player."
18. I try to keep my lunch breaks as short as possible so I can be most productive at work.
19. If I have to work late, or on a weekend, I usually don't mind.
20. The most productive employees are those who focus on their job regardless of how long it takes.
21. Many people foolishly sacrifice their personal lives for work success.
22. I have never been called a "workaholic."
23. I admire people who are orderly and tidy at work.
24. Work is the most important thing in my life.
25. It's unrealistic to expect an employee to work hard every single day.
26. People who know me describe me as very dependable when it comes to keeping appointments.
27. Sometimes, I have a lot of difficulty getting started in my job.
28. I envy people who can take early retirement from work.
29. I daydream about vacations a lot.
30. I often lose my focus on the job.

Generally, such personality-based measures show a lower predictability of worker dishonesty than do overt measures. Nevertheless, many companies find such instruments to be valuable in making hiring decisions that embody more than assessing whether a particular applicant is likely to steal from them. Indeed, in the next chapter, we will look specifically at the Big Five approach to personality and its growing relevance for the workplace.

Were Diogenes alive today, he would perhaps still be in search of the truly honest person. But instead of wandering mockingly through daylight Athens (or Chicago, Paris, Hong Kong, Tokyo, or São Paulo, for that matter) with a lantern, he might well be administering a psychological test.

9

Measuring Emotional Intelligence and Stress

In the search for optimal productivity, the fields of management, human resources, and organizational development have undeniable fads. Increasing competitive pressure, accelerated by globalization, has brought a sense that if only we could scientifically discover and mine some long-overlooked aspect of human performance, our treasure would be immense. From "Theory Z" and "quality circles" all the way up through "reengineering," the past two decades have witnessed a succession of hype-surrounded managerial topics. Though many have possessed definite value, almost none have been able to sustain their initial enthusiasm.

Undoubtedly, emotional intelligence has been among the most euphoria-generating of these in recent years. Propelled like a bombshell by Dr. Daniel Goleman's 1995 bestseller, *Emotional Intelligence,* followed three years later by his *Working with Emotional Intelligence,* the subject has exerted continuing impact. Such a reaction, of course, is hardly surprising, in view of the claims made for this previously obscure dimension of employee functioning.

For instance, Dr. Goleman has asserted, "The rules for work are changing. We're being judged by a new yardstick: not just by how smart we are, or by our training and expertise, but also by how well we handle ourselves and each other. This yardstick is increasingly applied in choosing who will be hired and who will not, who will be let go and who retained, who passed over and who promoted . . . No matter what field . . . [these rules] measure the traits that are crucial to our marketability for future jobs . . . [and focus] on personal qualities such as initiative and empathy, adaptability and persuasiveness."

Is emotional intelligence really so important, or just another fad destined for the same forgotten fate as so many others? Though prognosticators seem most successful when, like Nostradamus, they offer their predictions in an impenetrable blur, it seems clear that what Dr. Goleman and his colleagues have identified is indeed emerging as a key element of workplace success. In an economy now dominated by work teams and interpersonal change, our prospect for achievement appears more and more linked to his emphasis on "managing ourselves and handling our relationships more artfully." But how is this precisely to be done?

The search for personal characteristics, other than IQ, that adequately explain variation in success is hardly new. As far back as 1920, Dr. Edward Thorndike, "dean" of psychometrics in the United States, developed the concept of *social intelligence* as a means of identifying noncognitive aspects of individual accomplishment in various attainment outcomes. But such groundbreaking work was eclipsed by the predominance of behaviorists who were influenced by John B. Watson in the 1920s and 1930s, and then by the growth of cognitive psychology in the post–World War II era. Professional interest in a comprehensive view of intelligence languished until the late 1980s, when theorists, led by Harvard academician Howard Gardner, sparked the "Multiple Intelligences" approach.

In Gardner's influential view, we each have a spectrum of intelligences clearly distinguishable from cognition and its measurement in the form of IQ. Basing his view on neurological and physiological findings, Gardner insisted that adults and children vary significantly in their verbal, arithmetic, aesthetic, kinesthetic, and social capacities, and that contemporary education badly needed to incorporate such findings. Similarly, his colleague, Robert Sternberg at Yale University, found evidence among managers at Fortune 500 companies, that what he called "practical intelligence" appeared to account for at least as much on-the-job success as did intellectual prowess. Certainly, Sternberg's research seemed intuitively sensible—nearly all in organizational life have met highly intelligent people who failed to realize managerial success, despite their scholastic accomplishments and SAT scores. And conversely, we frequently hear of tremendously successful CEOs, but who utterly lack an impressive academic background.

Recently, such theorists as Robert Baron and Gideon Markham at Harvard University have argued that social skills, akin to what's been dubbed *emotional intelligence,* also play a key role in determining entrepreneurial prowess. Alluding to recent physiological research, they suggest, "A substantial body of evidence indicates that people who are high in such social skills as impression management and enhancing their personal appearance induce higher levels of positive moods or feelings in others than people who are lower in such skills. Other research indicates that positive affective states can strongly influence judgments and decisions, making these more favorable."

So what personality traits specifically are involved? Setting aside the possible existence of business-related intelligences, separate from *both* intellect and emotion, it seems reasonable to argue that, for example, managerial success depends on certain qualities that psychologists ought to be able to identify and measure accurately.

After all, almost everyone in a large organization knows of supervisors or executives who run meetings well, smoothly persuade subordinates to "go the extra mile," and keep team projects to planned deadlines—and, conversely, those in identical positions with most likely the same (or an even higher) IQ who run meetings poorly, alienate and antagonize subordinates, and inevitably fail to meet projected deadlines for team accomplishment.

However meaningful, such anecdotal impressions can be notoriously difficult to translate into a psychometric format. For one thing, does the highly effective manager know precisely why he or she is so successful? How about the one who's highly unproductive? It's not unusual for people at work to take personal credit for team efforts when it's hardly justified, or to blame others for their own interpersonal shortcomings. As one academic researcher jokingly commented at the latest Academy of Management annual conference, "Asking people to rate their own emotional intelligence, like empathy or social sensitivity, may be as useless as asking them to rate their own physical attractiveness. Nobody is really going to be objective."

Is third-person or 360-degree assessment the obvious psychometric solution, then? Definitely not. For nearly 100 years, psychologists have recognized the power of the *Hawthorne effect,* in which well-liked employees are given inflated scores by supervisors on all sorts of unrelated personality traits like innovativeness, reliability, attentiveness, or even honesty.

For this reason, Goleman cautioned in his groundbreaking book that, "Unlike the familiar tests for IQ, there is as yet no single pencil-and-paper test that yields an 'emotional intelligence' score, and there may never be one." Similarly, Charles Steiner, in *Achieving Emotional Literacy,* observed, "The term EQ—a measure of emotional intelligence—though snappy, means less than you might think. It is a marketing concept, not a scientific term. An emotional quotient can't be measured and scored like an intelligence quotient . . . we can meaningfully speak of EQ as long as we don't claim to be able to measure it precisely."

While the absence of robust and well-validated tests of emotional intelligence is currently lamented, an intense effort is underway to develop precisely such measures—for certainly, if the topic retains organizational "staying power," it will bring its creators considerable status, influence, and financial reward. Currently, various popular publications have presented ways to assess emotional intelligence among managers, supervisors, and job applicants; most such instruments, however, lack any semblance of acceptable scientific validation.

Among the most cogent researchers have been Drs. Victor Dulewicz and Malcolm Higgs at England's Henley Management College. In the past several years, the two have developed both a compelling conceptual model and a specific instrument, the Emotional Intelligence Questionnaire (EIQ), worthy of close attention.

Generally supportive of Goleman's viewpoint, Dulewicz and Higgs agree that emotional intelligence in the workplace comprises specific attributes, or *competencies,* and that these can be assessed and fostered through well-planned training programs. They emphasize that although the existing research basis for emotional intelligence is chiefly educational and physiological, the concept offers organizational benefits and is especially valuable for understanding managerial behavior and learning. While insisting that emotional intelligence is developable, they concede that evidence is unclear as to which stages in life are most amenable to skill-based training.

Paralleling Goleman's work and others, Dulewicz and Higgs have identified the following seven competencies:

1. *Self-awareness.*   The awareness of one's feelings and the ability to recognize and manage these
2. *Emotional resilience.*   The ability to perform well and consistently in a range of situations and when under pressure
3. *Motivation.*   The drive and energy to achieve results, balance short- and long-term goals, and deal with challenge and rejection
4. *Interpersonal sensitivity.*   The awareness of the needs and feelings of others, and the ability to use this awareness effectively in interactions and decision making
5. *Influence.*   The ability to persuade others to change their viewpoint
6. *Decisiveness.*   The ability to use insight and arrive at a decision when faced with ambiguous information
7. *Conscientiousness.*   The ability to display commitment to a course of action, and to act consistently and ethically

Based on this conceptual model, Dulewicz and Higgs first published the EIQ in 1999. For psychometric validation, they drew heavily upon subscales of the well-established 16 PF and Occupational Personality Questionnaire, and determined that the EIQ possessed significant validity and reliability. Comprising 69 items on a five-point Likert scale, the EIQ yields seven subtest scores and an overall *emotional quotient* (EQ). Though research and application with the EIQ are still in infancy, it shows promise as a reliable way to measure workers' emotional intelligence and provide a psychometric basis for training programs aimed at building on strengths and overcoming weaknesses.

As highlighted in chapter 3, the *Big Five* approach to personality study has gained decisive influence in the past decade. With roots over a century old in Sir Francis Galton's taxonomy of English-language personality traits, this model suddenly flowered after the utter doldrums of personality study in the 1970s and 1980s when many academicians despaired of ever creating a truly scientific field.

But now, hundreds of studies have confirmed that human personality can be meaningfully understood—and measured—on five broad, distinct dimensions. Though different researchers use slightly varying terms, these encompass: (1) emotional stability, (2) extraversion, (3) agreeableness, (4) conscientiousness, and (5) openness to ideas and experience. Cross-cultural research has repeatedly affirmed the validity of this model, though interestingly, there's evidence for a sixth dimension—involving sensitivity to social harmony and "maintaining or saving face"—measurable among those in Asian cultures.

The Big Five model has spawned two major tests, both of which are increasingly used in the workplace and which provide valuable light on workers' emotional intelligence: (1) the Neuroticism Extraversion Openness Personality Inventory—Revised (NEO-PI-R) and the (2) Hogan Personality Inventory (HPI). Because of their respective length (each has over 200 questions), their use seems most suitable for employee development and training, rather than screening job applicants.

Published by Drs. Paul Costa and Robert McCrae in 1992, the NEO-PI-R comprises 5 major scales [(1) neuroticism, (2) extraversion, (3) openness, (4) agreeableness, and (5) conscientiousness] and 30 subscales. These subscales include such conceptually meaningful categories as gregariousness, excitement seeking, aesthetics, achievement striving, and deliberation. All scores are analyzed separately according to the respondent's gender, and cross-cultural variations have also been found.

With 240 items presented on a five-point Likert format, the NEO-PI-R is time-consuming and laborious, especially for those without high literacy skills. Reflecting these practicalities, as well as the more intrusive nature of items of neuroticism, the authors devised a new test, the NEO-4, which is identical to the NEO-PI-R, but deletes the entire neuroticism scale.

The NEO-PI-R's scales of extraversion and agreeableness seem particularly relevant to assessing social skills. Though systematic studies have not yet been undertaken, the subscales of warmth, gregariousness, and positive emotions (pertaining to extraversion) and trust and altruism (relating to agreeableness) seem highly pertinent to qualities of emotional intelligence identified by Goleman, Dulewicz and Higgs, and others. Recent research shows that we react most favorably to those who display demonstrably positive moods.

The other major test to emerge from the Big Five personality model is the Hogan Personality Inventory (HPI), published by Drs. Robert and Joyce Hogan in its current form in 1992. Like the NEO-PI-R, the HPI is currently among the most time-consuming instruments relevant to the workplace; it comprises 206 items in true-false format. Carefully formulated to avoid potentially running afoul of EEOC guidelines on adverse impact, the HPI contains no items relating to sexual preference or religious beliefs, nor does it include questions about the respondent's possible criminal offenses, drug and alcohol incidents, or racial and ethnic attitudes. Finally, there are no items regarding physical or mental disabilities.

The HPI comprises seven primary scales: (1) adjustment, (2) ambition, (3) sociability, (4) likability, (5) prudence, (6) intellectance, and (7) school success. Each of these is divided into several subscales, comprising 41 in all. The largest of these is the adjustment scale, which contains eight subscales; the smallest is the school success scale, which has only four. The test also includes a validity, or lie, scale.

The most pertinent HPI scales assessing social skills are the sociability, and especially the likability, scales, with the key subscales comprising entertaining, easy to live with, sensitive, caring, and likes people. Emerging from what the Hogans call *socioanalytic theory,* which "assumes that people are motivated in a deep biological sense to engage in social interaction," the HPI focuses more strongly than does the NEO-PI-R on interpersonal traits. With a viewpoint especially relevant to understanding the roots of emotional intelligence, the Hogans comment that, "People's social behavior is regulated by two broad and usually unconscious motives. The first . . . impels us to seek the acceptance and recognition of our peers—and to try to avoid their criticism and rejection. The second . . . impels us to seek status and power relative to our peers—to try to avoid losing status and control."

It's crucial to note, however, that the most important Big Five predictor of job performance, across a wide variety of managerial and technical settings, is that of *conscientiousness,* not extraversion or agreeableness. Surprisingly, it's a relatively new construct, one which didn't exist independently even a generation ago; yet, this is also now viewed as basic to emotional intelligence.

Like all other personality traits, conscientiousness is understood as encompassing several aspects: feeling self-competent, being orderly, respectful of supervisors and accepting of prescribed routines, striving to achieve goals, maintaining adequate self-discipline, and being deliberate rather than impulsive.

Can we learn to be more *conscientious* if it's not our natural bent? The psychological evidence moderately suggests *yes,* though such major traits never change overnight or without significant practice and effort. For this reason, job applicants who score low on conscientiousness, typically as measured by specific subscales on covert integrity tests, are unlikely to be hired. Seen from another light, though, employee training programs on time management or "clutter elimination" are predicated on the implicit view that we can certainly learn to become more orderly, tidy, and organized, aspects that underlie conscientiousness.

Stress and Burnout

Unless you've arrived from another planet lately, you know that workplace rage is a major concern in today's organizational world.

Such phrases as *going postal* (describing an employee on the rampage), *road rage,* and *air rage* have all become new additions to the English language. Research clearly shows greater rage among employees than ever before; indeed, workplace violence was recently rated the main threat to America's largest corporations, according to a survey of Fortune 1000 security executives. The Workplace Violence Research Institute, based in Palm Springs, California, has estimated that on-the-job violence specifically costs employers at least $36 billion annually, up *850 percent* over the last five years. The U.S. Department of Justice estimates that those victimized at the workplace comprise 500,000 employees who lose an average of 3.5 days of work per crime.

As a result, companies are putting major effort into screening out potentially enraged, violent employees. Under the legal doctrine of *negligent hiring,* firms' recruiters are potentially liable for the harmful actions committed by those they've brought on board. By failing to administer appropriate personality tests to assess for violence proneness—or so the current legal argument goes—such enterprises are guilty of negligence, just as they would be for allowing incompetent contractors to install a defective elevator system that later malfunctions and injures employees.

Can you really alter an angry personality through counseling or therapy? The experts themselves aren't sure, though a client's actual motivation for change is paramount. For instance, it's known that the teenage killers at Columbine High School successfully completed an anger management course as a consequence for their earlier antisocial behavior. Yet, at the same time that they were participating in this course, the two were actively plotting their school's horrific destruction.

Probably more common on the job than rage in the new, information age economy, both in the United States and abroad, stress has become pervasive. Due to corporate downsizing, many employees are working longer hours than ever before, and in an increasingly competitive global marketplace, the slack that was once common (remember the era of leisurely lunches at relaxing restaurants?) has almost completely disappeared. A return to the pre-

Internet pace of doing business seems as likely as the triumphant reemergence of typewriters, carbon paper, slide rules, or black-and-white television. We're all getting more and more wired, even elementary school kids with their beepers, screen names, and e-mail accounts.

Psychologically speaking, therefore, nearly everyone is facing more stress at work these days. Company presidents, executive managers, and senior administrators certainly know this to be true, because they're experiencing it themselves. The question for job recruiters, therefore, isn't whether the candidate will have to deal with occasional on-the-job stress, but how emotionally stable and strong one is to cope with it regularly. It's highly expected—virtually guaranteed—nowadays that we'll be encountering potentially stressful situations almost daily involving deadlines, long hours, high-pressure meetings, and few opportunities to really unwind.

Can we learn to cope with stress more effectively if that's not our *forte?* Absolutely. Over the past decade, a substantial body of medical and psychological research has emerged to show that nearly everyone can learn to handle job tensions more effectively, though we differ in what particular activities are most pleasurable. One point to keep in mind: people benefit more from structured stress management programs, such as associated with a health club or employee assistance program, rather than from "winging" it individually and without supervision.

At present, two of the most widely used instruments focusing specifically on stress measurement are the Maslach Burnout Inventory (MBI) and the Occupational Stress Inventory-Revised (OSI—R). Both are typically utilized as part of stress reduction programs, rather than in screening job applicants. That is, preemployment testing for stress tolerance, similar to assessment of conscientiousness and honesty, is typically conducted via covert integrity tests.

Initially published in 1981 when the term *burnout* first entered the popular English language, the MBI reflected Dr. Charles Maslach's research on the nature of emotional exhaustion in human services work and education, and its potentially devastating consequences for caregivers, clients, family members, and others. Though *burnout* had become almost a buzzword, it had generated little systematic theory or empirical data. Along with others pioneering in the field, Maslach and his colleagues recognized the need for a standardized measure of an individual's experience of this psychological phenomenon.

Emerging from the original MBI-Human Services Scale, the MBI—General Scale (MBI—GS) is likewise self-administered and takes only a few minutes to fill out. Sixteen items are presented on a six-point Likert scale. The same three subscales were retained for the MBI—GS. Research with a wide variety of international samples, including Dutch civil servants, and Canadian, Finnish, and Polish health care professionals, established adequate reliability and validity.

At present, the MBI is the subject of research aimed at better clarifying the relationship among the three subscales—(1) emotional exhaustion, (2) depersonalization, and (3) personal accomplishment—as well as in establishing international norms for burnout among different populations.

The OSI—R, originally developed by Dr. Samuel Osipow in 1981, is a broader instrument; it is therefore a potentially more useful instrument than the MBI. The OSI—R assesses three broad dimensions of work-related adjustment: (1) occupational stress, (2) psychological strain, and (3) coping resources. For each of these domains, scales measure the individual's or environment's specific attributes pertaining to work-related adjustment. The OSI—R comprises 140 items on a five-point Likert scale. Significantly, all scores are different, depending on the respondent's gender.

Occupational stress is measured by six subscales collectively, called the *Occupational Roles Questionnaire*. These encompass (1) role overload, (2) role insufficiency, (3) role ambiguity, (4) role boundary, (5) responsibility, and (6) physical environment. Psychological strain is composed of four scales, called the *Personal Strain Questionnaire*, reflecting affective, subjective responses of various types. For the person who is unable to cope effectively with various stresses on the job or elsewhere, strain can be classified into four chief categories: (1) vocational strain, (2) psychological strain, (3) interpersonal strain, and (4) physical strain. Finally, the *Personal Resources*

Questionnaire is composed of four scales pertaining to one's coping resources: (1) recreation, (2) self-care, (3) social support, and (4) rational and cognitive coping.

Just as the NEO-PI-R and HPI are quite useful for measuring facets of emotional intelligence, these two instruments, both derived from the Big Five model, also possess strong utility for assessing stress tolerance. On the NEO-PI-R, the neuroticism scale offers key signs of emotional distress, particularly the subscales of anxiety, angry hostility, depression, and vulnerability. It has been found clinically that those who score high on these four subscales often work less effectively due to inner turmoil.

As for the HPI, the adjustment and ambition scales are clearly the most relevant indicators. Indeed, drawing exclusively from 25 items taken from these two overall scales and five subscales, the Hogans have devised a stress tolerance scale with high validity and reliability. They relate to such emotional factors as anxiety, depression, calmness, and even-temperedness.

Whether emotional intelligence will prove to be the "philosopher's stone" for transforming lead into organizational gold remains to be seen. Too many managerial fads have come and gone for a touch of cynicism (or is it just a strong dose of reality?) not to be appropriate. And acquiring potent social skills may not be as learnable as some optimistic theorists currently believe.

It's undeniable, though, that more and more work today is being organized and conducted in teams, as well as in multiethnic if not international, contexts. For such reasons, those who are best able to interact conscientiously, empathically, and dynamically with others are certainly most likely to succeed. In developing the most effective preemployment screening and training programs, psychological assessment will be increasingly crucial.

10

Do You Use Your Problem-Solving Style?

Productivity has become a supreme buzzword nowadays. So what's the most effective way to accomplish a task or project at work? We all differ psychologically in our preferred methods, don't we? Is it better to rely upon our personal strengths or to confront our weaknesses? Is it just a matter of casual taste, or do people really vary significantly in their problem-solving styles? And, what about work teams? Are they affected by our individual tendency to forge the future, or rather preserve the past, to get things done? Why do particular employee mixes generate synergy, and others disaster? Is it simply due to how well they *like* each other?

Until recently, psychological testers gave surprisingly meager attention to addressing such crucial job-related questions. The explanation is undoubtedly multifaceted, but almost certainly reflects their overriding emphasis on personality, emotions, and cognition, as the main bases for all achievement. Of course, these aspects are important; our cooperativeness, motivation, and intellectual abilities exert a strong workplace impact.

But the focus only on personality and cognition has badly ignored a third, and definitely separate, dimension of human performance. For too long, it's been unexplored both conceptually and methodologically. Fortunately, the situation is now changing. The impetus of global competition has impelled managers and executives to begin recognizing and capitalizing upon our individual, problem-solving styles. To a degree difficult to imagine a generation ago, they're awakening to the realization that this third way offers a huge opportunity for enhancing individual and group productivity.

Intriguingly, psychologist Abraham Maslow was among the first to affirm the existence of this little-known facet of human potential. As we'll see more closely in the next chapter, his seminal studies of high-achieving men and women, those whom he called *self-actualizers,* revealed their distinguishing feature not to be sheer intellect or unbridled self-esteem, but rather their ability to fully use their potential to accomplish goals. That is, far more than others in their particular avocations, they were able to apply their talents in real tasks and solve real problems.

Specifically, though, how did they do this? As Maslow explained, it was by knowing, trusting, and, above all, acting upon their particular innate nature: "They listen to their own voices . . . They find out who they are and what they are . . . They find their own biological natures, their congenital natures, which are irreversible or difficult to change."

Shortly before his death in 1970, Maslow became convinced that this inner, biologically based "core" had wide implications for employee productivity in teams—and this was probably even more important than emotional and social factors. "Good individuals can form a lousy group," he memorably asserted. "I have worked with people who I *hated,* so long as they were good workers. It's not really essential that we love each other in order to work well."

The Kirton Adaptation-Innovation Inventory

As an astute theorist, Maslow knew that he was on the proverbial right track. He did not live long enough, however, to embark on empirical work to substantiate his notion of problem-solving style and its relevance for individual and group accomplishment. Indirectly, that torch has been passed to two particular organizational consultants: Dr. Michael Kirton and Kathy Kolbe. Working independently in England and the United States, respectively, each has developed a powerful testing system that builds significantly on Maslow's initial insights. Both stress employee problem-solving tendencies, as opposed to camaraderie or cognitive ability, as instrumental for success.

Dr. Michael Kirton, a British industrial psychologist, is undoubtedly the most prominent figure in this assessment domain. His Kirton Adaptation-Innovation Inventory (KAI) has generated hundreds of published studies and organizational applications, especially in Europe and Asia. Currently director of the Occupational Research Centre in Berkhamsted, England, Kirton has jokingly reminisced, "I remember vividly, as a boy of six, an occasion when two loved and respected relatives 'fell out' because each had been sorting out some matter, in their different characteristic ways, which clashed. Each muttered darkly that the other side was 'silly.' I remember saying to each one: 'Oh! Uncle isn't being silly and he always does it this way.' For some reason, the memory stuck."

Flash forward several decades. The discerning six-year-old had become a business consultant seeking to implement change in a Midlands company faced with its unavoidable necessity. While some managers eagerly thrived in this situation, others were obviously floundering; to Kirton, the explanation had nothing to do with their motivation or intelligence. Clearly, they all wanted the firm to excel, and they were all cognitively capable.

Positing the existence of a third variable relating to job achievement, Kirton insisted that everyone can be located on a continuum ranging from an ability to "do things better" to an ability to "do things differently." He labeled the two ends of this continuum *adaptive* and *innovative*, respectively.

Kirton identified *adaptors* as workers characterized by precision, reliability, methodicalness, and prudence. They tackled problems by effecting incremental improvements with increased efficiency, and with minimum disruption to prevailing organizational structures. In contrast, *innovators* typically challenged the status quo, had little respect for past custom, and sought radical change and redefinition of problems. Neither was better than the other; they simply approached problems in crucially different ways.

In 1977, Kirton published his KAI in Britain, and from the outset, it has attracted considerable professional interest. The KAI comprises 32 items with a five-point response range, yielding a theoretical mean of 96 and a total range of 32 to 160. One's total KAI score comprises three interrelated subscores: (1) *sufficiency of originality,* (2) *efficiency,* and (3) *rule/group conformity.* Generally, these can be closely predicted from the overall score, but roughly one-third of respondents show small but significant variations among the subscores.

1. *Sufficiency of originality.* This helps to demark differences among people in their preferred handling of original ideas. Adaptives generally produce a smaller number of new concepts; almost invariably, their notions are "close to the vest" and fit preexisting structures. In contrast, innovators offer bold or fresh ideas that frequently challenge existing ways of doing things. Their notions often appear brilliantly unconventional, or else impractical and hare-brained, in ways that adaptors' mainstream notions never do. "The more innovative often also have problems in choosing among the ideas they proliferate and picking one that pays off," Kirton has observed. "Evidence suggests that they are more likely to fancy their more innovative ideas, whilst adaptor assessors will be more likely to choose the innovators' less innovative ideas as worthier of support."

2. *Efficiency.* This subtest aids in differentiating people's preferred method of problem solving. Adaptives typically define problems carefully and tightly, noting precedent, searching methodically for relevant information, and arranging data in orderly ways. By working closely with the prevailing system, adaptives are more likely to get it to work for them, and to use their creativity to refine, order, improve, and make more immediately efficient current structures and paradigms.

   Innovators trade off the immediate benefits of efficiency and lower risk by focusing on the big picture. Less meticulous and detail oriented, they strive to tackle problems by stepping outside conventional patterns of accomplishment. "It is difficult at times," Kirton concedes, "to see the high innovator as efficient, operating with what, by most people's standards, is a lack of consistency, predictability, and key detail. Yet, this is the most efficient way of producing something different, as distinct from something better. Innovative efficiency is the best way to break the paradigm—when that should be needed."

3. *Rule/group conformity.* This subtest helps to distinguish styles in managing structures within which problem solving occurs. Adaptors abide by rule conformity for the structure it provides, and they accept group conformity to ensure collaboration and cohesion. Essentially, they place a high value on form and order. Innovators, on the other hand, are more likely to solve problems by bending or breaking organizational rules; they have little regard for structure and tradition. Kirton thus observes, "For those who cherish rules . . . [innovators are apt] to often appear as abrasive, disturbers of the peace, undependable, and unnecessarily challenging to consensus."

By now, you've probably been tempted to guess your own score on the KAI and its three subtests concerning ideas, problem solving, and management. Is this actually possible to do? Research clearly demonstrates that it is, and people are fairly accurate, too, in estimating the KAI scores of their coworkers. So the test has definite construct validity.

A variety of international studies, likewise, indicates that innovators are prevalent in such vocations as marketing, planning, human resources, fashion buying, and entrepreneurship, whereas adaptors predominate in fields like civil service, cost accounting, maintenance engineering, nursing, and plant and branch-bank management.

In Kirton's view, the KAI has considerable relevance both for placing employees in appropriate positions and for creating effective teams. For instance, workers who are assigned to tasks inappropriate for their problem-solving style are likely to experience considerable strain. As Kirton has noted, "Both adaptors and innovators need to operate within their own capacity . . . People are at their best when operating in their preferred mode . . . To work in a contrary mode is expensive in terms of stress."

As for using the KAI effectively in team building, Kirton has observed, "[Those] composed primarily of adaptors or innovators were very different in their style of working when presented with a problem on a team-building seminar. One team which included three highly innovative people found it extremely difficult to work together, with one innovative participant having to retire periodically from the group in order to cool down. This team produced a highly imaginative proposal as a solution to the problem, but grossly overspent their budget. As expected, the team which was primarily composed of adaptors produced a solution to the problem which conformed to the guidelines and was submitted on time. The content, however, was unexciting and had not made full use of all the available resources."

With the huge transformation occurring globally today in group work projects, the KAI is gaining particular attention for its team-building usefulness. For instance, research has found that the larger the gap between coworkers' scores on the KAI, the more difficult for them to collaborate and communicate; even a difference of only five points between two people or groups is noticeable over time. Therefore, *bridgers* are often needed, that is, workers who have intermediate scores within a group and can mediate (i.e., act as a bridge) among team members with major gaps (20 or more KAI points). As Kirton has insightfully emphasized, the optimal mix of innovators and adaptors is always dependent on the particular team's purpose.

Empowered by our self-knowledge on the adaptive-innovative dimension, can we alter our problem-solving style as measured by the KAI? Or is it more or less a permanent feature of our psychological makeup? The results of carefully done studies suggest that our position on the adaptor-innovator spectrum coalesces by late childhood (if not earlier), strongly resists change, and remains relatively constant throughout our lives.

Specifically citing the biologically oriented work of investigators like Dr. Robert Cloninger (highlighted earlier in chapter 2), Kirton argues that the KAI assesses a psychological facet that is probably rooted in our innate temperament and is genetically influenced. For example, individual differences with respect to exploratory behavior in response to novelty have been linked to a polymorphism in the D4 dopamine receptor gene.

The Kolbe Index

A second highly influential assessment tool for problem solving is provided by the Kolbe System, developed by organizational theorist Kathy Kolbe over the past decade. The daughter of the vocational testing pioneer, E. F. Wonderlic, Kolbe has presented her approach in two cogent books, *The Conative Connection* and *Pure Instinct,* with a third, *Workplace Liberation,* in progress. Though her psychological measures are just beginning to spark academic research, her roster of major corporate clients includes American Express, Arthur Andersen, IBM, Xerox, and Intel.

Similar to Kirton, Kolbe has generated her ideas, and related forms of assessment, from applied organizational work rather than academic theory. Based on over 500,000 individual datasets, she has amassed considerable evidence that our problem-solving tendencies are independent of intelligence, personality, training, and education, and are highly stable and resistant to change. In Kolbe's view, this realm involves "an executive function of [the] mind: something innate, action-oriented, subconscious, protective, definitely not learned, and clearly a necessity."

Whereas Kirton identifies a single continuum (i.e., innovator versus adaptor) by which all people can be assessed, Kolbe specifies four different modes: (1) fact finder, (2) follow thru, (3) quick start, and (4) implementor. These all refer to task accomplishment in everyday life: what we *do* to solve problems, challenges, and new situations, and not how we *feel.*

Thus, *fact finder* refers to the realm of probing and information gathering, *follow thru* to patterning and scheduling, *quick start* to innovating and risk taking, and *implementor* to physically demonstrating and constructing. These modes are all rooted in what Kolbe terms the *conative* (from the dictionary, referring to striving or volition) aspect of our mind.

The Kolbe System encompasses several assessment instruments. The foundation is the Kolbe A Index, evolving out of the Test of Creative Thinking over several years and refinements, as its author became convinced she was, indeed, measuring conation. On the Kolbe A, individuals are asked to choose one of four answers reflecting how they would be most—and least—likely to respond to 36 problem-solving scenarios.

For each of the modes—fact finder, follow thru, quick start, and implementor—the individual's scores are tabulated in a 10-interval scale that reveals one's natural tendencies to either: (1) initiate action, (2) respond to needs, or (3) prevent problems in that mode. Thus, Kolbe has identified 12 distinct *impact factors,* or problem-solving methods, seemingly universal. "While every individual can operate through all twelve methods, four—one in each action mode—are natural talents, or a person's innate abilities." The composite of these drives determines the individual's modus operandi (*MO*).

Kolbe emphasizes that our problem-solving domain is innate— and as such, is resistant to external attempts at change or modification. In this important context, conative functioning appears linked to mounting evidence on the role of biological *temperament* in human development. She suggests that individual variability among the impact factors is evidenced as early as infancy and is measurable by elementary school age. Her studies have decisively shown that employees' MOs are not significantly altered even through intensive training programs.

Like Kirton, Kolbe persuasively argues that employees are more productive both as individuals and team members when empowered to tackle tasks in their preferred style, and that strain and conflict result when thwarted from doing so. In her view, a great deal of workplace rage and stress, highlighted earlier in this book, stem directly from the frustrations that employees feel in being denied the opportunity to address problems in their own way.

Kolbe emphasized that individuals can be creative in any mode, and therefore, there is no "better" or "worse" score for one's problem-solving mode—quite unlike both cognitive and personality testing, in which a high IQ is certainly more desirable than a low IQ, and high self-esteem or achievement motivation is preferable to low self-esteem or low achievement motivation. For example, an insisting Fact Finder, who looks closely at historical facts and details, might be a huge asset on certain work teams, whereas a resisting Fact Finder would be advantageous for others. Similarly, accommodating fact finders could serve as effective bridges when gaps exist between individuals or groups.

Not surprisingly, Kolbe has directly tied conation to enlightened management theory, contending, for instance, that our striving instincts "propel us toward personal productivity [and] form the inner self that struggles for freedom, that cries out for self-actualization."

As predicted by Kolbe's theory, successful employees in similar jobs tend to have MOs that fall within a specific "range of success." In this regard, supportive data have been found for wide-ranging occupational groups, including accountants, attorneys, engineers, marketing managers, manufacturing salespersons, and commercial pilots. It should also be noted that MOs have been found nonassociated statistically with ethnicity, gender, and race, an important aspect that makes the Kolbe selection process unbiased by EEOC guidelines.

When utilized together, the Kolbe A, B, and C instruments have proven valuable for maximizing organizational productivity. By identifying one's particular MO (Kolbe A) and comparing it with one's perception of job characteristics (Kolbe B) and the supervisor's perception of it (Kolbe C), it becomes possible to determine "the right employee fit." Over the past decade, Kolbe has found that approximately 70 percent of employees in many organizations are in the wrong position for their MO—to the detriment of both personal and organizational productivity.

Kolbe stresses that her approach isn't aimed merely at career guidance, but perhaps more crucially, offers a means for enhancing work group functioning. Expanding upon Maslow's concept of *syn-*

ergy as the ideal (where the whole is greater than the sum of its parts, like a basketball team), Kolbe provides practical assessment of synergy's existence on a team through an Internet-accessible set of algorithms tied to performance with forecasting programs that have proven over 80 percent accurate in predicting profitability, on-time delivery, and other performance criteria.

Kolbe has analyzed a host of factors that undermine team success, including conflict, polarization, inertia, and loss of will. Such dysfunctional interrelations are almost inevitable unless conative factors are carefully balanced. As Kolbe explained in a recent management training seminar, "It doesn't really matter if you have an extravert and an introvert working together on a marketing project. These are personality traits, and if they offer any 'real-life' relevance, it's basically off-the-job; so, maybe the extravert and introvert won't become best friends.

"But the conative dimension is vital to on-the-job productivity, and therefore, it impacts on profitability. For example, if you pair an insisting Fact Finder with a resisting Fact Finder to implement a record-keeping system, or assign a trio of resisting Quick Starts to initiate a new marketing campaign, you're courting disaster. Why? Because in the first case, direct conflict will result, and in the second case, the group will sink into inertia. The potential for achievement is crippled."

When viewing a group in terms of Kolbe dynamics, it's first vital to assess: Is the group really a team? In the strictest sense, a group of people actually comprises a team when three criteria are met:

1. Members work collectively to achieve agreed-upon, measurable goals that are specifically assigned to the group.
2. Members are responsible to each other for their productivity.
3. Each member has influence in the group and makes a commitment to its goals. If each member's contribution is not merely valued, but vital for the decision-making process, all of his or her instinctive energy becomes available through commitment to the group.

Both Kirton and Kolbe astutely emphasize that a focus on cognition and personality has too long dominated assessment efforts. Rather, psychology has got to broaden its perspective as to what people do most effectively on the job in tackling tasks and finding solutions to problems. With a convincing track record in organizational intervention, this approach offers a fresh, "third way" of measuring and optimizing individual employee and team achievement.

11

Self-Actualization:
The Heights of Personality

Among the fastest-growing fields in worker assessment today is that of identifying and developing *peak performers*. Increasingly, managers are recognizing that employee motivation is a factor of huge importance in determining organizational success. Although quantifying individual and group motivation is still a rigorous task that psychometricians have yet fully to "crack," the decisive conceptual shift has already taken place.

For a host of economic, demographic, psychological, and social reasons, management by threat has essentially disappeared. Though sarcastic and demeaning bosses certainly still exist, intimidation isn't what it used to be. In an economy marked by unprecedented job shortages in both the private and public sector, how to attract and retain desirable workers (i.e., arouse their motivation) has become a top human resources priority. And, in this domain, the notion of self-actualization has become paramount.

No longer dismissed as impractical for its emphasis on personal creativity, values, and fulfillment, this outlook is most closely associated with the humanistic school espoused by psychologist Abraham Maslow. As discussed in chapter 2, he developed a model of human personality rooted in biology—but one that also recognized the impact of culture—that steadily replaced the older freudian and behaviorist conceptions.

His *hierarchy of inborn needs* argued that every person is born with certain *basic* needs encompassing the physiological, including needs for safety, belongingness or love, respect, and self-esteem. Comprising an unfolding hierarchy, these needs intrinsically demand satisfaction. When this occurs, then our higher need for self-actualization comes to the fore. "A musician must make music, an artist must paint, a poet must write ... to be ultimately at peace with [oneself]," Maslow influentially wrote in the mid-1940s. "What a man can be, he must be. This need we may call self-actualization ... It refers to [one's] desire for self-fulfillment, namely, to the tendency for him to become actually in what he is potentially: to become everything that one is capable of becoming."

Over the next quarter-century, Maslow argued increasingly that the workplace was a key domain of self-actualization for men and women whose "higher" motivations were dominant. He became convinced that just as renowned scientists, mathematicians, writers, artists, musicians, and educators experienced great fulfillment in their tasks, so, too, could all workers if allowed the opportunity to express their "core" personality unfettered. Maslow was also sure that the more fulfilled—and motivated—people are on the job, the greater their innovativeness and productivity. To move people up the motivational ladder from basic to higher needs was his goal.

Be all that you can be became the recruitment slogan of the U.S. Army in the post-Vietnam era, and it was chosen by no marketing or public relations accident. By the 1970s, Maslow's psychological outlook, albeit in simplified form, had an allure for millions of baby boomers, including those likely to enlist in the armed forces. It also had appeal for leading managerial thinkers like Peter Drucker and Warren Bennis, who saw that the hierarchy of inborn needs integrated all previous motivational approaches into a single coherent perspective. Maslow lived long enough to see his work embraced not only by business and governmental innovators; at the time of his death in 1970, he had also gained an international stature.

In the ensuing years, Maslow has become ever more influential as a "guru" of managerial theory, and his writings on individual potentiality are now evoking unprecedented interest in Japan, China, and other nations seeking rapid economic growth. All of this he accurately foresaw: "The old-style management is becoming steadily obsolete," Maslow contended more than a generation ago. "The more psychologically healthy [people get], the more will enlightened management be necessary in order to survive in competition, and the more handicapped will be an enterprise with an authoritarian policy . . . That is why I am so optimistic about [enlightened] management . . . why I consider it to be the wave of the future."

Measuring Self-Actualization

Such optimism is usually a good thing in business practice, but to what extent has the humanistic school produced useful ways to assess employee motivation? Significantly, Maslow himself never published, or even vigorously involved himself, in developing a measure of self-actualization. Nor did he serve as a mentor or consultant for such work. Especially in that Maslow had once been a founding figure in personality testing, his failure to develop such a potentially valuable inventory may seem surprising.

But not really. Though self-actualization theory offers an intriguingly upbeat and even inspiring image of personality, the task of creating accurate assessment tools has proven daunting for over 30 years. Many efforts have proven empirically unsuccessful. How so?

Well, think back to chapter 5 on test construction. Suppose we want to devise a scale that effectively screens out dishonest job applicants from their honest cohorts. To accomplish this goal, we must first demark relevant "criterion groups": employees identified as definitely *dishonest* versus those who are regarded as *honest*.

That's not a very difficult task. Virtually all companies maintain employee records (they'd be running big legal risks if they didn't), which invariably contain information regarding the reason for job termination. Once a large number of workers have completed a pre-employment integrity test, it's quite an easy matter one or two years later to compare overall test scores (as well as answers to specific items) among those who were later dismissed for theft, sabotage, or other forms of dishonesty (versus those who were never fired, or even disciplined, for dishonest conduct).

In today's business world, the most widely used measures of integrity have proven effective, though not at 100 percent accuracy, in separating the proverbial wheat from the chaff. The goal is to avoid hiring people who will "steal you blind"—whether in a department store, bank, or health care facility—and a test that can help do that is truly worthwhile. That's why corporate America is willing to spend tens of millions of dollars on such instruments. Makes sense, right?

Now, let's go back to Maslow's theory of self-actualizing men and women. To invent a worthwhile measure of self-actualization, it would first be necessary to identify employees at the peak of personal achievement versus those functioning at a lower level. But how do we define *achievement*? By salary? Supervisor ratings? Frequency of promotion? Self-described job satisfaction? Three-hundred-sixty-degree assessment? How about absenteeism or physical health—aren't those relevant, too?

Since Maslow never really viewed self-actualization as an *either-or* phenomenon, but rather as the apex of a pyramid-like hierarchy of motivations and corresponding needs, it would be even more useful to distinguish employees at *varied* levels of personal accomplishment. This requires additional categorization and differentiation of employees.

Is the process of assessing self-actualization now appearing more difficult than at first glance? Definitely. And, bear in mind: Maslow was never altogether clear in his writing whether self-actualization is totally an *inner* state of fulfillment, harmony, and satisfaction, or whether it also necessitates some *external* form of validation. For example, consider two lawyers, former classmates at law school, who are both 42 years old.

Marion is a junior partner in a prestigious New York firm, earns well over one-half million dollars a year, and has won major professional awards as a labor attorney. Well-known for taking on landmark cases, Marion rubs elbows with prominent politicians—and also routinely works 70 hours a week, with no time for hobbies, personal interests, or friends—let alone planning a family or doing community service.

Out in the suburbs, Alison has a part-time job as a legal temp while she helps raise her two young children. She also enjoys hiking with her husband, and she enjoys volunteer fund-raising for the local PTA. Alison also has many friends. Of course, she has won no professional awards and earns less than one-tenth of Marion's salary. Needless to say, she rubs elbows mostly with her kids' playmates when they're on the dining room floor.

So who's more self-actualizing, Marion or Alison? And who gets to decide? Does it depend on which one feels happier about her life, or who contributes more to society? And how do you measure either of *those* two variables? Would it change your opinion if you learned that Marion has become passionately in love (or, conversely, has been hospitalized with an ulcer), or that Alison's husband has just lost his job?

As readily evident, assessing self-actualization among workers is a lot more complicated than identifying those likely to shoplift, explode in rage, or work alone successfully for most of the day. Maslow himself understood this issue realistically; perhaps, this is why he never attempted to devise such a test. Nevertheless, he firmly believed that self-actualization *should* and *could* be assessed meaningfully.

Indeed, toward the end of Maslow's life, he outlined a brilliant, long-term study that, unfortunately, has never been carried out: each year, Brandeis University's (where he taught) entering freshmen would receive a full battery of personality instruments like the Rorschach and Thematic Apperception Test, as well as measures of self-actualization tendencies. Then, this same cohort would be psychologically reevaluated every 5 or 10 years for the rest of their lives. Such a longitudinal study would generate an unprecedented amount of scientific knowledge on the interrelationships of personality, intelligence, motivation, career achievement, life satisfaction, mental health, and even physical well-being and mortality.

For this research design, Maslow certainly was influenced by the work of Stanford psychologist Lewis Terman, whose research team tracked a group of intellectually gifted college students over many ensuing decades. Unfortunately, no social scientist has yet undertaken the truly ambitious psychometric project that Maslow envisioned in the late 1960s.

The most well-known test of self-actualization to emerge is the Personal Orientation Inventory (POI). Developed by California psychologist Everett Shostrom, it was first published in 1963 and remains a useful instrument. Especially in assessing employees on issues like job satisfaction and burnout, the POI has gained a definite following among organizational consultants. It's also popular in fields like education, health care, and recreation, which all have a strong service orientation.

Shostrom and Maslow were never personally close, partly because they lived on opposite coasts. They maintained a collegial relationship, however, and Maslow recommended the POI as a worthwhile, though certainly not definitive, means to measure self-actualization. He was convinced that psychology badly needed to develop such instruments in order for humanistic theory on *higher motivation* to be embraced by most managers and executives.

In essence, the POI consists of 150 two-choice comparative-value and behavior judgments. Items are scored twice, first for 2 basic scales of personal orientation (*inner-directed support* and *time competence*), and second for 10 subscales, each of which measures a conceptually important aspect of self-actualization. *Inner-directed support* refers to our ability to self-pilot through life constructively; *time competence* refers to our capacity to enjoy the present, as well as make meaningful plans for the future. In both Shostrom's and Maslow's view, these are vital features of self-actualizing people.

The POI's 10 specific subscales involve, respectively: (1) *self-actualizing value*, (2) *existentiality*, (3) *feeling reactivity*, (4) *spontaneity*, (5) *self-regard*, (6) *self-acceptance*, (7) *nature of man—constructive*, (8) *synergy*, (9) *acceptance of aggression*, and (10) *capacity for intimate contact*. Though abstract, such terms reflect the basic tenets of humanistic psychology that people at the peak of emotional health have a high capability of accepting themselves, expressing their emotions easily, taking personal responsibility for their decisions, viewing life in positive terms, and getting along with others.

If some of these attributes sound familiar, you're right: they underlie what organizational theorists today are calling *emotional intelligence*—although the POI omits traits pertaining to empathy, and also aims at measuring a more exalted form of personality. Particularly relevant in this context are the POI subscales for feeling reactivity, spontaneity, and capacity for intimate contact; it's unlikely that employees would be prized for emotional intelligence if they lacked awareness of their own feelings, an ability to communicate them, and a capability of achieving closeness with others.

Can the POI be faked to yield a higher self-actualization score? Ironically, research has shown that when individuals were asked to distort their responses in order to make a "good impression," they scored *lower* than otherwise on various POI subtests, including existentiality. For example, if presented with items like "I always follow the rules and standards of society" and "I sometimes reject society's rules and standards," fakers have been found to *agree* more than would ordinarily be expected.

What does this suggest? Apparently, that efforts at fabricating one's degree of self-actualization are counterproductive as measured by the POI, for most fakers will try to appear more conformist and rule-oriented, instead of more independently minded, in their mistaken belief on what self-actualization is all about.

Surprisingly, for a personality measure derived from Maslow's emphasis on the "heights" of personal fulfillment, the POI has no subscales for either achievement motivation or transcendence via peak experiences (i.e., spirituality). And, it seems a little top-heavy in emphasizing traits like self-acceptance and self-liking as key facets of emotional health. In this regard, POI items seem somewhat dated for certainly, American values on personal fulfillment have changed in the past 35 years.

Undoubtedly, the POI's orientation, as is true for all psychological tests since their inception more than a century ago, also reflects the unique blend of idiosyncrasies and biases of its developer. For this reason alone, if for no other, it's crucial to use more than a single test in employee assessment.

Are any other tests of self-actualization currently available? In Montreal, Dr. Richard LeFrançois and his colleagues at the Sherbrooke Geriatric University Institute have developed an instrument called *the Measure of Actualization Potential (MAP)*, which identifies successful and well-functioning individuals. Published in 1997, the MAP comprises 27 items, and it highlights the concepts of self-awareness and openness to experience.

Interestingly, research is underway in both Japan and China to develop up-to-date measures of self-actualization. At Ryukoku University in Kyoto, Professor Yoshikazu Ueda has devoted several years to constructing the Questionnaire of Healthy Personality, based explicitly on Maslow's concepts and currently used for educational purposes.

The eight dimensions that Ueda specifies are as follows: (1) integration, (2) self-objectification, (3) social adaptability, (4) social independence, (5) sentiment, (6) emotional stability, (7) self-control, and (8) spontaneity. Perhaps reflecting the interpersonal rather than individualist orientation accentuated in Japan, Dr. Ueda's measure of emotional health gives less weight to traits like self-esteem than does the POI.

Based partly on consultations with Professor Ueda and other Japanese psychologists and management consultants, I've recently developed a measure of self-actualization, known as the *Hoffman Inventory of Self-Discovery (HISD)*. Comprising 100 questions presented on a five-point Likert scale, it's predicated on Maslow's view that self-actualizing men and women have higher motivations and life goals than those seeking to satisfy basic needs for safety, belongingness, love, self-esteem, and respect. The HISD comprises 14 subscales, such as achievement motivation, initiative, novelty seeking, need for intimacy, and leadership, to name but a few. As a counseling tool, the HISD has proven useful in helping people better clarify their core values (i.e., what currently makes them feel most fulfilled on the job and whether important self-needs are yet unmet).

Another prominent Asian researcher of self-actualization theory and its employment application is Professor Xu Jinsheng of Beijing's Institute of Social Science. It's his viewpoint—one that Maslow strongly embraced at the end of his life—that for humanistic psychology to reach its full global potential, it must transcend Western, and specifically American, cultural values relating to work, such as individualism and materialism.

For example, Dr. Xu has argued that in China, as well as in certain other Asian countries, professionals who find themselves thwarted in satisfying a *basic* need (e.g., attaining a high salary or a spacious home) are often spurred to a higher motivational level involving self-actualization and corresponding traits of creativity, discipline, and intellectual accomplishment. Dr. Xu suggests, however, that in the United States, thwarting of the lower needs frequently causes employee despair and burnout.

What accounts for such important cultural differences in employee motivation? It's a totally new question, and one with major future implications for American and Chinese joint-managerial strategies. For the past few years, Dr. Xu and I have been developing a motivational model to successfully integrate both Eastern and Western concepts of worker self-actualization, so that organizations can assess and nurture it more effectively. Certainly, increased globalization in the coming years will only accentuate the need for such an approach—and for viable psychological measures of peak personality and achievement.

12

Spirituality: The New Frontier

Does your job give you a sense of meaning or purpose in life? A deep connection with others? What about intense happiness, joy, or bliss? In performing your day-to-day activities, do you ever feel empowered by something higher, even transcendent? Certainly, such questions would have seemed out of place, if not peculiar, in the organizational world not long ago, but an attitudinal sea change is underway.

At all levels today, from the mailroom to the boardroom, people are seeking precisely this higher dimension of work. Whether described as "inner fulfillment" or "finding God in the workplace," it's a domain attracting unprecedented interest. As never before, managerial consultants and psychologists are rushing to fill the void. Relevant assessment methods and training programs are much in demand. And while the trend may have originated in small family-run or faith-based enterprises (and initially been derided) it's now affecting major companies like Motorola and Xerox as well.

Both in newspapers such as the *Wall Street Journal* and professional opinion setters such as *The Academy of Management Executive* and the *Sloan Management Review,* commentators aren't ridiculing the subject anymore. For one thing, Equal Employment Opportunity Commission (EEOC) guidelines and related rulings have firmly upheld employees' rights to religious belief and practice—broadly defined now to include wicca and paganism.

Also, leading public figures such as Oprah Winfrey and Senator John McCain are touting their own spiritual journeys. At the very least, it may be lucrative to do so, for books on religion and spirituality (especially from a personal viewpoint) have become among the most profitable publishing categories. Likewise, there has been a fourfold increase in the number of religious radio and television programs in the past quarter-century, with continued growth readily apparent.

Gone from business articles are the sarcastic jokes about "California flakes" and the "granola and sandals crowd." On the contrary, the chief managerial concern now is how to address employees' spiritual yearnings most effectively, and yet avoid potential legal problems concerning those with differing beliefs, or none at all.

What is driving this burgeoning yet leaderless movement? Certainly, the causes appear numerous, ranging from the baby boomers' imperative for midlife soul searching to the globally sustained benefits of economic stability and Internet growth. Some observers insist that the United States is in the midst of a historically cyclical "religious revival" affecting many institutions besides the workplace. Other commentators emphasize job-related stresses wrought by widespread downsizing, reengineering, rampant high technology, and the disappearance of traditional career paths and ladders.

From this perspective, Dr. Sam Menahem, director of the Center for Psychotherapy and Spiritual Growth in Fort Lee, New Jersey, and the author of two books on prayer and counseling, has contended: "Many psychotherapy clients today complain that their corporate employment has created a spiritual vacuum in their lives. Through counseling, they seek to bring meaning into such employment. It's time for the corporate world to integrate spiritual values and meaning into the environments they create for their employees."

Such a sentiment is rapidly entering the mainstream. Corporate chaplains now number in the thousands, and represent a booming industry. The Academy of Management gave unprecedented attention to the topic of workplace spirituality in its 2000 convention; speaker after speaker highlighted the necessity for developing new ways of fulfilling workers' needs in this crucial realm.

Researchers also emphasized that while the subject of employee spirituality seems idealistic, it carries with it tangible benefits for organizations and individuals alike. For example, the evidence is clear that spiritual well-being is positively correlated with self-ratings of physical health and vitality. Likewise, individuals who score higher on measures of both spiritual and existential well-being are closer to their ideal body weight. Spiritual wellness has also been found to be positively linked with adjustment to both dialysis treatment and cancer-induced pain, and negatively linked to hypertension.

Dating back to Sigmund Freud's contemptuous view of religion as a crutch for the emotionally weak and immature, psychologists have tended to see spirituality in a negative light. But like so many other axioms of freudian thought, that notion is rapidly being dispelled, because research overwhelmingly shows the opposite is true.

Those who attend religious services regularly are not only physically healthier than the rest of the adult population, they're emotionally healthier, too. Individuals who pray regularly report greater happiness than the rest of the adult population. Likewise, people who score high on a scale of spiritual well-being report fewer symptoms of psychopathology such as anxiety and depression (the latter comprising the number one mental health problem in American society—more prevalent than all the others combined).

Research has also tied spiritual well-being to greater self-confidence, assertiveness, helpfulness, and praise giving: all prized elements of what's known in today's workplace as *emotional intelligence.*

The psychological effects are real and not trivial at all. Though few professionals suggest that spiritual wellness itself is a cure for tension, the data are indisputable that meditation programs for employees reduce the adverse effects of stress and also minimize burnout. If introduced only as a cost-effective way to lessen expenses associated with recruitment, selection, and absenteeism, spirituality-based programs have definite financial benefits to reap for organizations that sponsor them.

But how is that to be done, and what role does assessment play? As highlighted in a recent *Industry Week* article, CEOs exert a major impact when personally committed to this issue. Many are now publicly revealing their religious sentiments, and they are asserting that spirituality has not only helped them to be better people, but also more effective managers and leaders.

And yet, bringing spirituality into the workplace is no easy matter. First of all, how do we precisely define it? Confusion involving definitions has long been a stumbling block in producing effective techniques, but researchers today differentiate between *extrinsic spirituality* (typically involving formal religious belief and practice) and *intrinsic spirituality* (essentially involving privatistic attitudes and feelings, and not necessarily linked to one specific religion, or any at all). It's in this latter sense that programs, including such activities as guided meditation, yoga, Tai Chi Chuan, and mindfulness training will be involved.

Legal Considerations

After more than 35 years of exposure to equal employment opportunity (EEO) laws, employers in the United States are still struggling to understand and effectively deal with the challenges of employees' rights and needs in the workplace. It's an environment today that is much more diverse and dynamic than what was originally visualized by those who crafted the EEO laws.

Though religion was certainly addressed in the original laws, the primary focus was accommodation for religious observances outside the workplace: such as an observant Jew who could not work in a department store on Saturdays (the busiest retailing day of the week), or who insisted on wearing a yarmulke on the job. Such issues, though sometimes thorny from a legal perspective, were administratively straightforward.

Today's workplace brings much more heightened religious concerns to managers. For one thing, the advent of new technology, global competition, downsizing, and reengineering have created a growing number of employees seeking life value and meaning not only at home, but on the job. In addition, the huge, ethnic diversification of the American workforce has brought recent immigrants from the Caribbean, Latin America, India, Pakistan, the Philippines,

Bangladesh, and other nations with a more active religiosity than was previously the norm in many worksites.

Many supporters of this trend insist that employers can address legal considerations on religious accommodation in a meaningful way. For instance, a 1997 survey conducted by the Society for Human Resources Management (SHRM) reported EEOC statistics indicating that the most common form of requested religious accommodation provided for in 1996 was time off for religious observances: numbering almost three times those of the next most requested religious accommodation. The secondmost requested was display of religious materials, followed by requests for space and time for religious observance, study, or discussion during work breaks. Other requests involved wearing religious garb or jewelry at work and proselytizing coworkers.

The SHRM survey results were quite consistent with data provided by Fortune 1000 companies in a 1997 survey on diversity in the workplace. About one-third of the firms had diversity programs specifically addressing religious diversity; such methods included promoting a general awareness of religious diversity, discussing religious stereotypes, and conducting fair employment seminars in religion training on religious discrimination and accommodation.

It is interesting that 40 percent of company representatives believed that religious principles and values were an integral part of their organization's culture. While more than 85 percent reported that they provided reasonable accommodation for employees both to observe religious holidays and to wear religious symbols or garb, the majority reported no specific policy on employee religious study or prayer groups.

Historically, legal interpretations have required that employees requesting religious accommodation must meet certain tests relative to the sincerity and meaningfulness of their belief. The practice of spirituality through meditation, visioning, or spiritual contemplation has become increasingly prevalent in the United States work environment—yet, it has remained less controversial and less subject to regulation as an employee rights issue than formal religion. Ironically, those who practice a formal religion often want the same opportunities and rights provided to employees who practice non-sectarian (i.e., nondenominational) spirituality.

Assessment Instruments

In planning spiritually based programs, there's one key question: How can spirituality be best brought into the lives of workers? Psychologists such as Dr. Menahem, who are active in this field, emphasize that intrinsic spirituality training seeks to optimize individuals' sense of self-regard and also regard for others. "The emotion of hate, whether it involves hating oneself or hating another person, such as a family member, is often at the root of spiritual distress," he has observed. "It's therefore one of the first things that needs to be addressed. The other three root-issues are fear, guilt, and inferiority.

"The fear of success and the imposter-syndrome have particular workplace relevance, for many high achievers in the corporate world secretly feel inadequate and that they're imposters who will one day be ruthlessly unmasked for the incompetents they really feel themselves to be."

In collaborative work with Dr. Menahem and others, I've also found that spirituality development helps employees to feel a greater equanimity, physical vitality, connection with others, and ability to experience joy in ordinary aspects of daily life. To help nurture workers' sense of meaning and purpose and minimize burnout, what kinds of assessment tools are available?

Though psychological measures on spirituality have been used for more than a half-century, these have mainly involved religious cognition, faith development, lifestyle, and character. The Religious Orientation Survey, developed by the humanistic theorist Gordon Allport in the 1950s, is the best researched of these—and focuses on one's personal basis of religious activity or commitment. Although it's likely that such instruments are positively related to *intrinsic spirituality,* they're not highly relevant to workplace issues and may also run well afoul of EEOC guidelines. For this reason, there's greater organizational interest today in utilizing assessment tools with a broad, nonsectarian viewpoint.

Certainly, the most widely used instrument in this domain is the Spiritual Well-Being Scale (SWBS). Devised by Craig Ellison and Robert Paloutizian at the Alliance Theological Seminary in Nyack, New York, in 1976, the SWBS has spawned numerous studies in a diversity of settings, including universities and seminaries, clinics and hospitals, and even ski clubs and federal prisons. It's been used to assess professional women, military personnel, nurses, homemakers, college students and teenagers, hospitalized patients, the elderly, and evangelical Christians as well as atheists.

The SWBS was developed specifically due to the absence of any systematic, subjective quality-of-life measure that encompassed both religious and "core-value," or existential, well-being. The test consists of 20 items evenly distributed to comprise two subscales: (1) *religious well-being* (with items referring to one's sense of God) and (2) *existential well-being* (with items related to one's sense of meaning and purpose in life).

Both validity and reliability have been adequately established for the SWBS, and it has demonstrated a reasonable correlation with the Personal Orientation Inventory (POI), which measures self-actualization, highlighted in the previous chapter. In view of the importance of religion among the Hispanic community in the United States, it's noteworthy that the SWBS has been recently translated and validated in a Spanish version with high internal consistency and test-retest reliability.

Four other measures are worth mentioning in this context. Like the SWBS, they're mainly useful for employee seminars and discussion purposes—and definitely not for screening, selection, or promotional objectives. Thus, a promising new instrument developed by Professor Hamilton Beazley at George Washington University is the Spirituality Assessment Scale (SAS). Comprising 30 items, its author defines *spirituality* as "a faith relationship with the Transcendent" and focuses on spiritual traits specifically within organizational settings, such as honesty, humility, and service to others.

Research based on the SAS suggests that within organizations, spirituality seems to encompass three more-or-less separate dimensions: (1) a faith relationship with the transcendent, which Dr. Beazley calls *sacred spirituality;* (2) a *psychological spirituality,* which is similar to the first category but doesn't involve belief in the transcendent; and (3) *nonspirituality,* which is falsely presented as spirituality, and is neither spiritually nor psychologically true spirituality in terms of important personal traits.

The Spiritual Assessment Inventory (SAI) is a theoretically based measure of spiritual maturity from a Judeo-Christian perspective. As such, it may be perceived as discriminatory by those with differing religious or nonreligious perspectives. Designed by John Hall and George Edwards in 1996, the SAI comprises 43 items scored on a five-point scale. Although usefully seeking to measure the traits of spiritual maturity and awareness, as well as life quality, the SAI has unfortunately failed to achieve high validity and reliability; its Judeo-Christian emphasis, likewise, limits its usefulness.

The Index of Core Spiritual Experiences (INSPIRIT) was devised in 1991 by Leon Kass and four colleagues in the mental health field. It's aimed at assessing two core elements of spirituality: (1) experience(s) that convince an individual that God exists and (2) his or her perception that God dwells within. INSPIRIT is a short measure comprising seven questions; the first six are individually scored with differing response options for each, and the seventh has 13 parts, the last of which allows the respondent to describe personal spiritual experiences. With acceptable reliability and validity, the INSPIRIT scale, despite its brevity, has proven effective in assessing spirituality. Though the INSPIRIT offers utility in measuring an individual's core experience of God or a Higher Power, its use is correspondingly limited to those holding such beliefs.

The Spiritual Scale (SS) is a 20-item measure developed by Robert Jagers and his psychology colleagues, and it is uniquely designed to assess spirituality from an Afrocultural perspective. Constructively validated by identifying core elements of African spirituality such as beliefs in life after death and continuity with one's ancestors, the SS has shown adequate reliability and validity. Revealing statistically significant differences between African-American and European-American participants, the SS seems to address spirituality from the Afrocultural perspective for which it was designed. An interesting finding is that regardless of their cultural background, women score higher on the SS than do men.

Finally, it's important to recognize that the Myers-Briggs Type Indicator (MBTI) has been found relevant in spirituality assessment, alongside its other workplace advantages highlighted in chapter 7. Although the MBTI measures neither one's spiritual well-being nor one's religious activity, Peter Richardson convincingly argues in his book, *Four Spiritualities,* that it provides a valuable methodology for spiritual assessment and planning.

Each of the four major jungian "types" has a specific orientation, or *journey,* in life, Richardson asserts, and the MBTI enables us to understand better our own spiritual odyssey, as well as those of the other three. With obvious workplace relevance, he insists, "Each of the four spiritualities tends to gravitate to compatible settings for fullest support. While dovetailing with the other spiritualities—sharing spaces, programs, and spiritual practices with them—each also needs special contexts that accentuate its unique approach."

Richardson names these four disparate paths as (1) the Journey of Unity, (2) the Journey of Devotion, (3) the Journey of Works, and (4) the Journey of Harmony, respectively. The first, the Journey of Unity, is that of the intuitive thinker (NT), comprising 12 percent of the population and exemplified by Buddha and Albert Schweitzer—along with the vast majority of theology professors. The second, the Journey of Devotion, is that of the sensing feeler (SF), comprising 38 percent of humanity and represented by Muhammad and St. Francis of Assisi. The third, the Journey of Works, is that of the sensing thinker (ST), making up 38 percent of the population and typified by Confucius and Moses. The fourth type, the Journey of Harmony, is that of the intuitive feeler (NF), making up 12 percent of the population and exemplified by Jesus of Nazareth and the Indian writer Rabindranath Tagore.

Intriguingly, Richardson contends that each type has a particular spiritual emphasis (contemplation, compassion, social action, or self-actualization) and also a unique weakness in approaching life. Thus, extraverts can become overly shallow, introverts can become overly isolated, judgers can become narrow-minded and obsessive, and perceivers can become ungrounded and unfocused.

Though Richardson explicitly links self-actualization most strongly with the intuitive feeler, it seems clear, however, that Maslow viewed "peak achievers" as encompassing a broad range of lifestyle qualities, interests, and even biological temperaments. He never related self-actualization to a particular jungian type; indeed, Maslow condemned those he sarcastically called "navel-gazers" for a selfish preoccupation with their own feelings, aesthetic values, and moods.

Especially because of the widespread use of the MBTI in organizations today, Richardson's model suggests that business managers and executives (who are disproportionally sensors, thinkers, judgers, and extraverts) must allow those of differing types to find spirituality (i.e., meaning and purpose) in their work.

In our affluent society today, it has probably never been more accurate to assert that money is only a *dis*incentive—never a prime motivator in influencing our satisfaction on the job. In coming years, we'll surely see scientific validation on the connection between our spiritual well-being at work and our highest productivity, involving both mind and body. Undoubtedly, the task of assessing intrinsic spirituality will play an increasingly vital role in that domain.

13

The Way of Leadership

Do you have the *right stuff*? What exactly is the *right* stuff, anyway? Can you still have it if you're not an astronaut, a general, or a famous sports coach? Can you be a leader if you're a computer scientist, a biotech engineer, an international marketer, an educator, or an organizational consultant? How about an artist or a writer?

Currently, there are over 8000 books on leadership available, including lessons that we can glean from King David and Jesus of Nazareth; Ulysses S. Grant and his nemesis, Robert E. Lee; Lord Admiral Nelson; Abraham Lincoln; Theodore Roosevelt; Queen Elizabeth, I; Winston Churchill; George Patton; Dwight Eisenhower; Jack Welch and Bill Gates; coach Vince Lombardi and golfer Don Sanders; and the entire crew of *Star Trek*. A recent book also highlighted Winnie the Pooh, although it really focused on his management secrets. Who's next for a role model? Barney, the purple dinosaur?

Attila the Hun seems to have sparked the "leader lessons" genre a decade ago, and no end lies in sight. Was it his way of rising up after 1500 years to exact ultimate revenge on the West? Like all of us, Attila no doubt had his good points, but I'd be wary about working for any boss who looked to this bloodthirsty, power-mad, mass sadist for insights on running today's business. Are we really that starved for true examples of leadership?

The answer, unfortunately, seems to be yes. In their 1985 classic work, *Leaders: Strategies for Taking Charge,* USC Professors Warren Bennis and Burt Nanus declared, "Leadership is a word on everyone's lips . . . but no clear and unequivocal understanding exists as to what distinguishes leaders from non-leaders, and perhaps more important, what distinguishes *effective* leaders from ineffective [ones] and *effective* organizations from ineffective."

Writing only a few years after President Jimmy Carter had micro-managed his position to include scheduling the White House tennis courts, Bennis and Nanus astutely observed, "The problem with many organizations, and especially the ones that are failing, is that they tend to be overmanaged and underled. There is a profound difference between management and leadership, and both are important . . . The difference may be summarized as activities of vision and judgment—*effectiveness*—versus activities of mastering routines—*efficiency*."

As the old French adage has it, the more things change, the more they stay the same. Though Professor Bennis and his colleagues in various leadership training centers have produced 15 years' worth of material on the topic, the latest newspaper headlines decry the absence of strong CEOs in the United States today. Indeed, in their foreword to *Leaders'* second edition, Bennis and Nanus accurately remarked, "Many of our concepts—on vision, empowerment, organizational learning and trust, for example—are as valid as they were [initially]."

And yet, the fields of leadership training and assessment have made definite progress. A new, psychologically based model has emerged and generated solid research and widely used assessment instruments. Known as the *transformational leadership* model, it has gained dominance in the organizational development field.

For well over a century, most historians had espoused the Great Man perspective that heroic individuals, by force of their unique personal traits and drive, successfully motivated others to achieve as well. The classic aphorism was that "Leaders are born, not made." Reflecting the influence of powerful figures like Napoleon Bonaparte and Abraham Lincoln, who arose out of obscurity and poverty to shake the world, it seemed an indisputable view. Great leaders were like distant gods, whom we could celebrate and revere, but never hope to imitate.

By the early 1900s, a dramatic shift propelled by freudian theory took place. Even renowned historical figures, such as Leonardo da Vinci, became viewed as deeply flawed and troubled, filled with seething inner conflicts. The very notion of heroism or leadership seemed naïve. As the humanistic theorist Abraham Maslow insisted in the 1960s, this freudian-led shift had fostered an attitude of debunking and reductionism, which denied the possibility of admirable people worth emulating. "The deepest and most real motivations are seen to be dangerous and nasty," Maslow decried, "while the highest human values and virtues are [denigrated as] essentially fake."

Sharing this prevailing mind-set, some scholars of leadership denied that it really existed. For them, history revealed that such achievement was totally accidental: a matter of being "in the right place at the right time." Most espoused only a slightly less extreme and cynical view: there is no such thing as overall leadership, only whether a person has the particular traits needed by a specific organization, at a specific time, for a specific task. From this vantage point, figures such as Abraham Lincoln, Franklin D. Roosevelt, Queen Victoria, Mahatma Gandhi, or Dr. Martin Luther King were leaders only because they were thrust into greatness by historical forces that can never be duplicated; that is, the *times* required a Lincoln, a Gandhi, or a Dr. Martin Luther King, and so they led powerfully.

The huge fallacy of this seemingly reasonable view, of course, is that it rests totally on hindsight—don't the times often *lack* a person who could make all the difference? As the joke among futurists declares, "Predicting the past is easy; it's predicting the future that gets hard." Neither Lincoln nor Gandhi nor Dr. King was inevitable. Just think of the Middle East today and its absence of effective leadership. Don't countless, promising, would-be leaders in business or politics fail miserably? The times-create-the-leader view also fails to present a psychological model for comprehending how leaders function in organizations.

During the 1980s, the pendulum finally began to swing back, perhaps not entirely to the nineteenth-century leaders-are-born, not-made outlook, but definitely into a centrist position. And what is it?

First, it rejects both antileader schools of thought, which either deny altogether the existence of leadership, or else regard it as situation-specific and unrepeatable. Second, the new model also rejects the earlier leaders-are-like-unknowable-gods perspective.

Rather, the consensus among managerial thinkers and organizational consultants is that certain personality traits, or *competencies,* are definitely linked to successful leadership, and almost all workers can improve their leadership capability by following scientifically validated methods.

Today, the transformational leadership model popularized by Bennis and Nanus is now dominant. While there are still academicians who criticize the concept of leadership as hopelessly "fuzzy," both management researchers and trainers are now focusing increasingly on means to assess, strengthen, and reward leadership traits. Hundreds of studies support the view that those who possess leader-linked qualities are more likely to be effective, in virtually any organizational setting, than those who lack them.

What are these traits? Though theorists for 15 years have disagreed on particular emphases, the following three are definitely the most salient: (1) possessing a broad vision (i.e., preferring to think in big-picture terms, as opposed to concentrating on minute details and micromanaging issues), (2) having excitement and optimism about the future (this seems obvious enough, for it's probably impossible to inspire employees if you're bleak or even indifferent about the future), and (3) valuing individuals for their unique talents and seeking to maximize their self-actualization as the building blocks of organizational success.

Three additional traits are often mentioned, too. These include: (1) dedication and hard work, (2) integrity, and (3) providing clear directives and specific feedback to subordinates. Certainly, these latter three aspects are important; however, they seem basic to all effective supervision and management, rather than unique to leadership.

A seventh, far more nebulous trait, is sometimes additionally suggested: charisma. Though charisma is obviously germane to some organizational settings, it's clear that many successful leaders in both private industry and the public sector are *not* charismatic, and that some who possess charisma, such as entertainers and athletes, are not necessarily leaders at all.

In any event, the transformational leadership model has clearly gained the ascendancy today. In the influential *American Psychologist,* published by the American Psychological Association, Bernard Bass in 1997 declared, "Evidence supporting the transactional-transformational leadership paradigm has been gathered from all continents except Antarctica—even offshore the North Sea. [This] paradigm is sufficiently broad to provide a basis for measurement and understanding that is as universal as the concept of leadership itself. Numerous investigators point to the robustness of the effects of transformational and charismatic leadership."

Assessment Measures

The field of leadership training is relatively young. At present, however, several assessment devices have gained wide usage in the organizational world. Among the most popular tests is the Multifactor Leadership Questionnaire (MLQ 5 X). Developed by Bernard Bass and Bruce Avolio at Binghamton University's Center for Leadership Studies in 1995, it has generated nearly 200 studies, and has been translated into Arabic, Chinese, French, Hebrew, Korean, and Thai.

Rooted solidly in the transformational leadership model, the MLQ 5 X comprises 45 items presented on a five-point scale. Its six dimensions of leadership comprise: (1) intellectual stimulation, (2) individualized consideration, (3) contingent reward, (4) management by exception, (5) laissez-faire, and (6) charisma. The MLQ 5 X exists in two forms: first-person (self) and third-person (other).

A variety of studies have shown the MLQ to be effective as an assessment tool in leadership training programs. These have involved settings as diverse as savings banks, community action agencies, offshore oil platforms, the United States Army, Chinese state-run industry, and the Israel Defense Force infantry.

In the latter study, conducted by Tsila Dvir at Tel Aviv University, a true field experiment found that according to their company leaders' and followers' MLQ ratings, platoon commanders who had undergone the transformational leadership training were more dynamic and active than a comparison group. Also, in contrast to the comparison group, the platoons led by those trained in transformational leadership had a greater sense of self-efficacy and belonging, and were higher in four of six measures of objective performance six months following training.

A second widely used measure is the Leadership Practices Inventory (LPI). Devised in 1990 by Drs. James Kouzes and Barry Posner at the University of Santa Clara, the LPI emerged from research that they conducted on leadership characteristics shown by a wide range of individuals, including managers, administrators, salespeople, homemakers, military officers, priests, teachers, and carpenters.

Conceptually, the LPI was strongly influenced by the transformational leadership model, for its researched starting point was the intriguing question: "Describe an experience in which you got something extraordinary accomplished in an organization, in which you felt you had led, not managed, your project to plateaus beyond traditional expectations."

Based on their survey results with over 1200 respondents, Drs. Kouzes and Posner identified five vital dimensions of leadership: (1) challenging the process, (2) inspiring a shared vision, (3) enabling others to act, (4) modeling the way, and (5) encouraging the heart. On the LPI, each of these dimensions is assessed via six items, thus producing 30 questions in all. Each question is answered on a 10-point scale, ranging from "almost never" to "almost always." Both first-person and third-person forms exist. Due to its ease of administration and practicality, the LPI has been especially useful in leadership training activities.

A third measure was originally designed by California psychologist Dr. Will Schultz in the late 1950s as a measure of social orientation: the Fundamental Interpersonal Relations Orientation-Behavior (FIRO-B). Though the test fell into obscurity in the 1980s and early 1990s, it has acquired new attention for its relevance to leadership assessment and training.

The FIRO-B stems from Dr. Schultz's view that beyond our basic needs for physical survival, shelter, food, and warmth, we each have unique interpersonal needs that motivate us. These needs encompass three different social dimensions, which Dr. Schultz termed *inclusion, control,* and *affection.*

Inclusion refers to how much we typically include other people in our daily lives, as well as how much attention and recognition we want from them. *Control* relates to how much influence and responsibility we want, and how much we want them to lead and influence us. *Affection* involves how close and how warm we are with others, as well as how close and warm we want others to be with us. Comprising 54 items presented on a six-point scale, the FIRO-B measures two factors concerning each need—(1) expressed and (2) wanted—and therefore yields six different subtests as well as an overall interpersonal needs score.

As a tool for assessing leadership ability, the FIRO-B's strength lies in its emphasis on the social dimension. Not only are the six subtest scores helpful for revealing details about our styles of social interaction, so, too, is the pattern among the various subtests.

For example, when expressed scores are higher than wanted scores, a potential leader would be oriented to taking action first and show little action anxiety. Such persons like to get directly involved, see how others react, and then express and reassess their actions. When wanted scores are higher than expressed scores, the prospective leader is comfortable about letting others act first and take the initiative. Likewise, while a potential leader might prefer to dominate and direct others as evidenced by a high control score, that he or she might avoid confrontations quickly if the total need score for inclusion or affection is higher.

Organizational consultants have found such insights valuable in grooming prospective leaders. Nevertheless, the FIRO-B focuses on only one personality trait relating to leadership and ignores others that are salient in the transformational leadership model, such as vision, enthusiasm, and empowerment. It's therefore important to use the FIRO-B with differing instruments, such as the Myers Briggs Type Indicator, when assessing and training for leadership.

Yet another recent, relevant instrument is the Global Transformational Leadership scale (GTL). Developed by Dr. Sally Carless, along with Alexander Wearing and Leon Mann, at Australia's Monash University and the University of Melbourne, respectively, the GTL scale is based explicitly on the transformational leadership approach. Its authors emphasize seven broad dimensions, comprising (1) communicating a broad vision, (2) fostering staff growth through new skills and opportunities, (3) providing individualized encouragement, (4) empowering employees in decision making, (5) introducing innovative ideas and methods, (6) serving as an effective role model by exuding self-confidence and consistency, and (7) projecting charisma (i.e., the combined qualities of trustworthiness, integrity, and ability).

Intriguingly, Dr. Carless asserts that while charisma may be the most difficult trait to assess and develop, it probably constitutes the most vital element of transformational leadership, and it is an important predictor of leader effectiveness, work performance of managers, and business unit performers.

In view of its newness and paucity of supportive research, the GTL scale's chief virtue undoubtedly consists of its brevity. Presenting a single question in third-person format concerning each of the aforementioned traits, the GTL scale comprises just seven items on a five-point scale. It can certainly be administered in under five minutes.

Research suggests that the measure successfully differentiates between managers who are high and weak performers, highly effective versus less effective in mentoring, and highly motivating versus less motivating. As Dr. Carless and her colleagues suggest, the GTL scale has definite usefulness both as a tool for management selection and promotion, and for use as an objective feedback instrument in leadership training programs.

As we head into a global era of unprecedented technological and economic change, the commodity of leadership will become ever more valuable. To thrive, grow, and excel, organizations of many kinds will, by sheer necessity, support those who can steer a course marked by vision, enthusiasm, and empowerment. In the task of selecting, promoting, and training leaders, psychological testing will undoubtedly exert a major impact.

Attila the Hun may always have his fans—or Barney the purple dinosaur, for that matter—but the field of leadership will increasingly turn to scientifically generated theory and methods of assessment.

14

Riding Change: Entrepreneurs and Expatriates

Though the "new economy" is a subject that is surrounded by undeniable hyperbole, the twin forces of globalization and high technology are transforming the way organizations have traditionally functioned. Unrelenting innovation in the quest for greater productivity is bringing change into the workplace as never before in modern history. To assess and develop workers' ability to cope with such change effectively has become increasingly important, especially concerning entrepreneurship and expatriate management.

In response, psychologists have turned their attention to measuring personality traits that are linked to entrepreneurial and expatriate success. As yet, this field of expertise is quite young, and methodologies are still evolving. But researchers active in both arenas are steadily amassing knowledge and applied methods for successful intervention.

Nearly everyone, it seems these days, wants to become an entrepreneur; surveys of college students in general, and specifically those planning to major in business, reveal that a sizable proportion intend to create their own firm, or join a start-up, rather than work their way up the increasingly nonexistent corporate ladder. Academic courses, degrees, training seminars, and funding sources devoted to entrepreneuring have burgeoned throughout the United States and abroad. Programs aimed at teaching entrepreneurial skills to teenagers are now taking root in many cities and suburbs. In its most recent annual convention, the Academy of Management devoted dozens of sessions to entrepreneurialism around the globe.

As an intellectual discipline, entrepreneurship has had a lengthy but narrow focus. In the early eighteenth century, Richard Cantillon coined this term specifically in reference to the economic function of risk bearing (concerning the buying of goods at certain current prices and selling them at future, uncertain prices). Jean Baptiste Say broadened the definition to include the notion of bringing together the factors of production. In 1911, the German economist Joseph Schumpter added the key concept of innovation in identifying entrepreneurial ability. He argued for the existence of many kinds of innovation, including process innovation, market innovation, product innovation, and even organizational innovation. Schumpter's seminal work also stressed the role of the entrepreneur in creating and responding to economic fluctuations.

Schumpter and his colleagues were economists, and the topic of entrepreneurship attracted minimal psychological interest until the post–World War II era. Psychometric study of entrepreneurial traits began with David McClelland's landmark research on achievement motivation. In this work, he relied heavily on the Thematic Apperception Test (TAT), a projective personality measure developed by colleague Henry Murray at Harvard University.

With this test, still widely used in clinical settings, individuals are shown a series of evocative pictures and asked to tell a story about each one. Based on the individual's narrative content (e.g., involving male-female conflict, emotional loss, rejection, or ambition), clinical psychologists can identify specific personality strengths and weaknesses. Because the TAT has never developed a rigorous objective scoring method but rather requires time-consuming individualized analysis, its organizational use has been sharply limited.

Using the TAT as a key personality measure, McClelland conducted a variety of studies involving children and adults in Brazil, Germany, India, Italy, Japan, Poland, Turkey, the United States, and other nations. Published in 1961, his influential book, *The Achieving Society*, argued for a strong link between achievement motivation and entrepreneurship—namely, "a similar interest in situations involving moderate risk or maximum opportunity of getting personal achievement satisfaction without running undue risk of failure."

Strikingly, McClelland also found that entrepreneurs in diverse countries shared two particular psychological traits regarding time that distinguished them from other businesspeople: (1) they were typically hustling and bristling with time pressure, and (2) they had an acute long-range perspective and ability to imagine the future.

"If people with a high need for achievement are to make good entrepreneurs, they should 'think ahead' more. In fact they do," McClelland observed. "They tell stories that deal more often with the remote future . . . They tend to anticipate a future event before it occurs. Their whole attitude toward time is so interesting in itself that it deserves extensive treatment."

McClelland's groundbreaking work caught the attention of theorist Abraham Maslow, who had long been interested in the personality traits of highly successful, creative men and women, those whom he called *self-actualizers*. During the 1960s, while engaged in managerial consulting in California's high-technology field, Maslow became convinced that the process of starting a new enterprise was a definite path of personal fulfillment—unleashing one's energy, skills, and creativity, and gratifying higher needs. Many successful entrepreneurs, Maslow suggested, were embarrassed to admit they were motivated by higher values involving societal improvement, justice, truth, or beauty, rather than amassing as much personal wealth as possible.

"The entrepreneurial function is too much underplayed and undervalued," he asserted in *Eupsychian Management*. "The entrepreneurial plan or vision, the recognition of a need which is being unfulfilled and which could be fulfilled to the profit of the entrepreneur and to everyone else's benefit [should] come under the general head of invention."

Since the work of McClelland and Maslow, organizational thinkers have recognized that business achievement is not synonymous with entrepreneurial ability. For example, those who successfully lead *Fortune 500* companies are not at all necessarily equally adept in starting new enterprises. Instead, a different and highly specific set of personality qualities seems to be involved; so much so, in fact, that business psychology studies have shown that it's possible to predict the long-term viability of start-up enterprises by knowing the entrepreneurial test score of their founders or leaders.

If not everybody is emotionally disposed to start a business from scratch, can the necessary traits be learned? After all, doesn't the recent growth of schools for entrepreneurship indicate that people can absorb the necessary attributes for success?

The answer is a qualified *no.* Through competent training, individuals can certainly improve their savvy and skills in matters of finance, marketing, and sales that intertwine with all types of firms, including start-ups. In this sense, schools of entrepreneurship have a definite role to offer would-be business founders. Psychological research has clearly revealed, however, that entrepreneurs possess certain specific personality traits—above all, the ability to take risks and to trust intuition—that cannot really be taught the way one teaches elementary accounting or brand-name marketing. Indeed, scientific evidence increasingly indicates that entrepreneurialism is genetically influenced or determined and, hence, even less likely to be learned than theorists earlier believed.

What forms of assessment are available to measure entrepreneurship? While no single personality test has yet emerged, several measures have been utilized to isolate and help predict traits associated with entrepreneurial success. These include the Miner Sentence Completion Tests, the aforementioned TAT, the Jackson Personality Inventory (JPI), the Edwards Personal Preference Schedule (EPPS), and the Myers-Briggs Type Indicator (MBTI). All have proven useful in helping to identify job applicants or employees with the qualities most closely linked to entrepreneurial prowess.

The most useful of these definitely appears to be the Miner Sentence Completion Test (MSCT), devised by Dr. John Miner, a psychometrician and organizational consultant specializing in entrepreneurialism. Based explicitly on McClelland's research on achievement motivation, Miner has advanced a model for 20 years that conceptualizes four distinct types of entrepreneurs: (1) the personal achiever, (2) the super salesperson, (3) the real manager, and (4) the expert idea generator. The MSCT also empirically differentiates among these four types by means of personality tests.

"Many people believe that there is an entrepreneurial personality—that certain kinds of people can struggle through to entrepreneurial success, whereas others cannot. And research supports this view." Miner has written, "But why do some entrepreneurs fail in one venture only to succeed in another? Why do some entrepreneurs initially succeed in a venture but fail when their firm reaches a certain size? First, there is not a single type of entrepreneur, but rather, there are four different types, each with a distinct personality. Second, each type of entrepreneur must follow a distinct career route to succeed, and each must relate to the business in a different way."

Of Miner's various instruments, the Miner Sentence Completion Scale—Form T, developed in 1986, has been most prominent as an entrepreneurial assessment tool. It comprises 40 items on a three-point Likert scale, and encompasses five relevant dimensions: (1) self-achievement, (2) avoiding risks, (3) feedback of results, (4) personal innovation, and (5) planning for the future. Also frequently used is the Miner Sentence Completion Scale—Form P, which is constructed in exactly the same way but contains different items. Its five scales include: (1) acquiring knowledge, (2) independent action, (3) accepting status, (4) providing help, and (5) professional commitment.

As mentioned earlier, McClelland utilized the TAT as his chief psychometric instrument, finding in the 1950s that entrepreneurs have high needs for both achievement and power, but low affiliative needs (i.e., relate to coworkers and be liked by them). Consistent with Miner's theory on the existence of different entrepreneurial types, the TAT has proven accurate in identifying technological entrepreneurs: those who exhibit moderate, rather than high, needs for achievement and power—and low needs for affiliation. As measured by the TAT, such entrepreneurs are strongly oriented toward independence and are concerned with meeting challenges more than financial rewards.

The JPI is a widely used personality test that measures such characteristics as innovation, conformity, organization, responsibility, and risk taking. When administered the JPI, entrepreneurs score higher than other people with regard to personal energy, risk taking, autonomy, reaction to change, and social adroitness; they score lower on measures of conformity and interpersonal effectiveness.

Another instrument used to assess entrepreneurialism is the EPPS, published in 1959. Objective and reasonably reliable, it requires respondents to rank-order the importance attributed to the fulfillment of emotional needs. The EPPS suggests that needs are ranked not in an absolute hierarchical structure as Maslow suggested, but uniquely by individuals, according to their personal priorities. When forced to choose among the fulfillment of various needs, the EPPS implies, people will select the need with the strongest motivating power for fulfillment.

Organizational use of the EPPS indicates that entrepreneurs exhibit high needs for achievement, autonomy, dominance, and change—and correspondingly lower needs for abasement, affiliation, deference, and order. As measured by the EPPS, the strongest reason for starting a business is the need for autonomy.

Using the EPPS, Professor Jean Lee at the University of Singapore conducted an interesting study of female entrepreneurs. Though entrepreneurship in Singapore had increased significantly for both genders in the past 20 years, its increase was larger among women. Results from the EPPS showed that women entrepreneurs possessed higher needs for both achievement and dominance than average women, and that autonomy and affiliation were less significant personality traits.

Finally, the MBTI has also been used in assessing entrepreneurialism. Research indicates that compared with managers, entrepreneurs are more likely to be intuitive, thinking, and perceiving; that is, managers are more typically sensing, feeling, and judging. Again confirming the existence of different personality types of entrepreneurs, technological entrepreneurs were more likely to be extraverted, intuitive, thinking, and perceiving than other scientists and engineers.

Conceptually intriguing for its relevance to entrepreneurialism is the Proactive Personality Scale (PPS), developed by Drs. Thomas

Bateman and Michael Crant in 1993. Focusing specifically on one's proactive, or self-initiating, tendency in life, its shortened version contains 10 questions on a seven-point Likert scale. With research already linking high scores on this important work-related trait to salary, promotions, and career satisfaction, the PPS's utility in predicting entrepreneurial ability seems likely.

With growing evidence on the link between personality and entrepreneurialism, we'll undoubtedly see an increasing use of tests adapted to pinpoint those with entrepreneurial capability. As highlighted in chapter 10, measures of problem-solving style such as the Kirton Adaptation Inventory and the Kolbe Index A are already being utilized in this way.

Expatriate Success

Another rapidly emerging area of workplace assessment relates to expatriate employment. Dating at least as far back as the ancient, Mediterranean-roaming Phoenicians, mercantilists have been willing to relocate in quest of profits. History is replete with examples of success, as traders not only expanded their wealth but exported their culture as well. Indeed, some scholars argue that cosmopolitanism, tolerance, and enlightenment are all direct products of expatriate activity over the centuries.

Yet, history is also littered with the dismal failures of enterprises unable to relocate successfully. Some collapsed utterly, or proved incapable over time, in adapting successfully to expatriation. *Why* this is so has become a question today of far more than academic interest. Globalization, accelerated by the phenomenal growth of the Internet, has forced more and more organizations to think and function internationally. The trend has accelerated tremendously in the past decade: surveys show that nearly 80 percent of midsize and large companies currently send professionals abroad. Despite the increased use and importance of international assignments, many firms, especially in the United States, have encountered significant difficulties in running the process adequately.

The stakes are high. A spate of recent studies identifies the overt failure rate (i.e., the premature return of an expatriate) from 25 to 40 percent for American managers. This rate is three to four times higher than that experienced by European and Asian international managers. Undeniably, the more effective an organization is in directing employee relocation, the greater are its productivity and financial reward.

The stakes are extremely high, for expatriate failure is associated with many costs. The direct cost of failure has been estimated at $250,00 to $1.25 million per employee, depending on job position and the nature of the assignment (e.g., duration, foreign location, and family situation, including the presence of school-age children).

In addition to such direct costs, there are potentially much greater indirect penalties, such as loss of employee self-esteem, self-confidence, and prestige among peers, as well as reduced motivation and unwillingness to provide support as a mentor, trainer, and social supporter for other expatriates. At the corporate level, indirect costs may result in reduced profitability for the foreign subsidiaries due to decreased local morale, lost opportunities for creating or penetrating markets, and relational difficulties with host-country stakeholders.

But the damage that is caused by expatriate failure is even broader. The negative effect when an expatriate returns home before completing the assignment is clear enough. But how about when he or she *remains* in the host country, but has nonetheless failed to adapt successfully to its culture? Externally, such employees are still on the job, but internally, research indicates, their motivation dwindles and apathy reigns. Losing self-esteem and self-confidence, the expatriate blights potentially successful relations between home and subsidiary firms and employees. The root cause? Almost invariably, it's directly the result of poor selection and training, and in this domain, psychological assessment has gained increasing organizational attention. Reflecting the newness of this field, specific tools are just beginning to be utilized.

Among the most intriguing is the Cross-Cultural Adaptability Inventory (CCAI), devised by Drs. Colleen Kelley and Judith Myers in the San Diego area and published in 1992. Though the CCAI is just beginning to generate significant research, it offers considerable conceptual relevance concerning expatriate success. As the test manual explains,

> The CCAI was not developed to predict success or failure in cross-cultural interaction. Instead, after learning about cross-cultural adaptability and examining their own assets and liabilities in this area, individuals who take the instrument can make decisions about their own readiness to interact with people from other cultures. They can also make choices about seeking further training to acquire the skills they need to be cross-culturally effective.

With adequate reliability and validity, the CCAI comprises 50 items on a six-point Likert scale and assesses cross-cultural adaptability on four respective dimensions: (1) emotional resilience, (2) flexibility and openness, (3) perceptual acuity, and (4) personal autonomy.

The emotional resilience scale focuses on our ability to cope with stress and ambiguity, accept and rebound from imperfections in oneself and others. The flexibility-and-openness scale measures the extent to which we enjoy the different ways of thinking and behaving that are typically encountered in cross-cultural experiences. The perceptual acuity scale focuses on our communication skills, particularly our capacity to accurately interpret subtle cues, both verbal and nonverbal, across cultures. Finally, the personal autonomy scale measures the extent to which we've developed a personal system of values and beliefs that enables us to feel confident to behave in unfamiliar settings, and to respect the perspective of others. Essentially, this scale deals with personal identity and empowerment in the context of unfamiliar environments and differing values.

Though the CCAI yields a total score, which is the most reliable indicator of an individual's cross-cultural adaptability, the measure is too global for training purposes. Rather, scores on the four specific scales are deemed more important for predicting adjustment and serving as the basis for programmatic intervention such as counseling.

A second instrument developed specifically for expatriate assessment is the Global Awareness Profile (GAP). Published in 1998 by Dr. Nathan Corbitt, a communications professor and consultant at Eastern College, the GAP is a test of factual knowledge rather than personality qualities. It comprises 120 questions in a self-scoring format that gives individuals a graphic representation of their global awareness.

The GAP measures our knowledge of six disparate geographic regions: Asia, Africa, North America, South America, the Middle East, and Europe. It also assesses cognition with regard to six different subject areas: (1) culture, (2) environment, (3) geography, (4) politics, (5) religion, and (6) socioeconomics, along with 12 questions on broad global issues. Like the CCAI, the GAP appears too new to be meaningfully applied as a selection tool, but rather is most currently valuable as a pretest to measure employees' readiness for expatriate work.

In view of the paucity of psychometric measures to predict expatriate success, I've recently developed the Hoffman Cultural Adaptability Scale (HCAS). Comprising 54 questions on a five-point Likert scale, the instrument encompasses four dimensions that are conceptually and empirically linked to cross-cultural adaptability: (1) risk taking, (2) travel orientation, (3) extraversion, and (4) affability. Each is measured on a separate subscale; a lie scale has also been incorporated. At present, norms for the HCAI are being amassed with respect to Chinese, Japanese, Indian, Korean, Pakistani, Russian, and South American expatriates currently residing in the United States. Exploratory findings already suggest that cultural factors that are related to the expatriate's country of origin may play a much greater role in adjusting successfully to U.S. life than have previously been recognized.

Interestingly, the Big Five model of personality assessment, highlighted in chapter 9, has proven helpful in predicting successful managerial expatriation. In a recent study, Maxine Dalton and Meena Wilson at the Center for Creative Leadership examined the performance ratings of Arab expatriate managers as assessed by both host-country and home-country supervisors. For the home-country supervisor, the Neuroticism Extraversion Openness Personality Inventory—Revised (NEO-PI-R) scales of conscientiousness and agreeableness were found to be significantly associated with performance ratings; agreeableness as a predictor of expatriate effectiveness has been found in earlier research involving German managers working in South Korea.

In a similar study conducted by Professor Paula Caligiuri at Rutgers University, the Hogan Personality Inventory (the other major Big Five test) was administered to American expatriates, mainly technical employees, from a large multinational company based in the United States and working in 25 different Asian, European, and South American countries.

The dependent variables were the expatriate's desire to terminate the assignment and his or her supervisor-rated performance. Similar to the findings of Dalton and Wilson using the NEO-PI-R, the higher the employee's score on extraversion, agreeableness, and emotional stability, the more likely his or her desire to continue the foreign assignment. Interestingly, the only one of the Big Five traits to relate to supervisor's ratings was conscientiousness.

Surprisingly, in neither study involving the Big Five dimensions was the openness scale related to expatriate success. It may well be that this scale assesses mainly cognitive or intellectual openness, as opposed to perceptual acuity. Another possibility is that different aspects of openness, such as openness to people and new experiences, are involved in productive expatriate work than what the NEO-PI-R and Hogan Personality Inventory currently measure. As such, additional ways to identify employees who are high on such qualities are decidedly necessary.

In today's swiftly changing workplace, successful entrepreneurs and expatriates will require formidable ability to ride the waves of change effectively. The pace of activity and the need for flexibility and vision have never seemed as globally crucial as they are today. It seems certain that psychological assessment will exert an increasingly vital role in these domains.

15

Going Global: Assessment in Greater China

Peta Cameron McAuley
The Chinese University of Hong Kong

Psychological testing is truly becoming an international force in the workplace, and among the most important regions of growth is that of greater China (Hong Kong, mainland China, and Taiwan) today. The Chinese people, of course, have a long history of association with the concept of objective assessment. The tradition of imperial examinations dates back to the Sui dynasty, around 1400 years ago. Those wishing to serve as officials in the imperial bureaucracy sat for examinations on a variety of subjects including literary style, familiarity with the Confucian classics, as well as competency with the characters used in writing and mathematics. Elegance of writing style and a good memory were the main qualities required for success in these examinations.

With the rapid growth of capital economies in Hong Kong, Taiwan, and, most recently, China over the last three decades, utilization of Western managerial practices, including modern objective assessment techniques, has steadily increased. Two important trends can be identified: first, Western assessment technologies have been imported mainly from the United States and Great Britain and adapted for use by Western-managed businesses and multinational corporations. For historical reasons, the predominant influence in Taiwan has been American, and British influence prevails in Hong Kong. At present, Hong Kong continues to act as an important springboard for Western technologies being launched into mainland China.

However, there is also a second growing trend toward local research and development of "indigenous" assessment tools by local Chinese psychometricians within Hong Kong, Taiwan, and mainland China. These instruments are currently used primarily by locally managed organizations, but they represent an important additional resource for Western-managed businesses that understand their potential contribution.

Today's businesses that operate in greater China and seek to use objective assessment techniques for recruitment, promotion, or development are faced with complex choices. The implications of adapting tests designed in the West as opposed to developing tests locally have been debated at length among leading personality researchers, such as Professor Michael Bond of the Chinese University of Hong Kong. As with most complicated issues, no wholly right or wrong answer exists.

For multicultural, multinational organizations, there are definite practical advantages in using well-designed instruments, such as the Myers-Briggs Type Indicator (MBTI), that have demonstrated both reliability and validly across a range of cultures. Such instruments allow for direct comparison between individuals from different cultural backgrounds, although undoubtedly at the cost of losing the possibility for more refined measurement of subtle cultural idiosyncrasies. Whenever people from different cultures are required to work together, the use of a common psychological instrument provides a benchmark for comparison and discussion of employee similarities and differences.

However, when assessments are to be made of indigenous people who will mainly work only with other indigenous people, whether from Hong Kong or southern China for example, a strong case can be made for the advantages of locally developed measures. For such measures are much more sensitive to cultural-specific factors that may strongly affect coworker relationships, teams, and hierarchical interactions. For example, in many Asian countries, such as China and Japan, the importance of maintaining and saving face is a key social value rarely as salient in Western nations such as the United States. For example, while Western-designed personality measures give little attention to a manager's sensitivity on this dimension, it might well have major consequence concerning his or her achievement in the Asian workplace.

Whether an organization chooses to use pancultural (*etic*) instruments or locally developed indigenous (*emic*) instruments, the same questions should always be asked about their technical soundness, because psychological measures always vary in their accuracy and reliability. For one thing, it's important to clarify that the test indeed measures the construct that it's designed to assess. For instance, if we're interested in measuring behavior at work (e.g., conscientiousness or leadership ability, a key question is: Does evidence exist that scores on that test predict relevant performance criteria?

As discussed in chapter 4, there's evidence in the area of personality measurement that situational-specific items (e.g., those directly linked to work contexts) are more effective than situational-nonspecific ones when it comes to predicting employee performance. Such issues apply to all psychometric instruments. However, there are ample reasons for being especially cautious when selecting instruments to be utilized in a variety of languages across the range of Eastern and Western cultures.

Before users can benefit from the application of pancultural instruments for making comparisons among individuals from diverse cultures, the test developer must first demonstrate that the various versions of the instrument are equivalent—linguistically, conceptually, and metrically. That is, to be culturally sensitive and relevant, items not only need to be translated accurately, but frequently adapted as well to local contexts. As suggested earlier, if we restrict item content to work situations, the likelihood of measurement error decreases. Technical checks on item loadings, factor structure, and predictive validity all provide evidence that alternate versions of the same test are indeed equivalent.

Currently, the international test development and consultancy firm of Saville and Holdsworth Ltd (SHL) offers the most comprehensive range of pancultural assessment tools adapted for use with Chinese people. SHL has been active in southeast Asia since the early 1980s and maintains offices in Hong Kong, Indonesia, Japan, South Korea, and Singapore. Following the British model of workplace assessment, SHL has an extensive range of assessment tools including ability tests, interest and motivation inventories, and personality questionnaires—most notably, the Occupational Personality Questionnaire (OPQ) and work simulation exercises.

The widely used OPQ is a series of inventories designed to measure work-related behaviors. Translated into Chinese, the Concept 4.2 version comprises 100 items, each with four statements from which those most true and least true or typical of the respondent must be selected. The OPQ includes 30 scales, grouped into nine factors within three realms: (1) relationships with people, (2) thinking style, and (3) feelings and emotions.

Somewhat different from the American model, SHL's policy is to train nonpsychologist, in-house line personnel to administer and interpret the assessment instruments. SHL's role is to actively monitor and support the professional use of their instruments through ongoing relationships with their clients, backed up by formal license agreements. Clients actively participate in the continued development of new and existing instruments by providing access to relevant assessment groups on which new instruments are trailed and normative and other technical data are collected.

In addition to test development, SHL also specializes in the development of online products to support a wide range of human resources activities. Their latest generation of products is aimed at supporting organizations in developing career and job websites and, ultimately, facilitating online screening and assessment in a range of languages of candidates attracted locally, regionally, and worldwide.

SHL's Hong Kong office has been the cornerstone for development of instruments adapted for use with Chinese people. Hong Kong is particularly well placed because of its location, physically and culturally, midway between mainland China and Taiwan. The use of Chinese script typifies this polarization. Hong Kong and Taiwanese Chinese people use complex, traditional Chinese characters, while Chinese people on the mainland and in Singapore use a simplified, character script. Translations of tests for use in these different locations must adopt these different scripts. In addition, SHL has made considerable progress in accumulating normative data on many of its tests, both in Hong Kong and mainland China, including the beginnings of regional norms centered on Guangdong, Shanghai, and Beijing.

SHL has been supporting psychometric testing in Hong Kong for over 10 years. Because of Hong Kong's history as a British colony until very recently and its position as a regional financial and business center, English continues to be an important medium of communication, particularly at midmanagement levels and up. Consequently, many Hong Kong clients choose to assess their graduate-level and managerial applicants in English. At the same time, particularly with the handover of Hong Kong to Chinese sovereignty in 1997, there has been a resurgence of Chinese national spirit and a concurrent push for greater use of Chinese language in the workplace. To address this demand, SHL is currently adapting many of its lower-level ability and personality instruments for use with Hong Kong Chinese. Information technology (IT) abilities and customer service personality traits are two popular areas currently assessed in Chinese within Hong Kong.

With the gradual opening-up over the last decade of Chinese markets, SHL has made steady progress in the adaptation of tests for use on the mainland. The Chinese government has sought to address the needs of foreign companies starting up new enterprises in China with such initiatives as the Foreign Enterprise Service Counsel (FESCO), which, among its other services, provides assistance in the recruitment of staff and workforce for new ventures. Many multina-

CASE STUDY 1

A large, multinational chemical company operating in China asked SHL to develop a competency model for midmanager levels and above. It was to be used in helping to train and develop local managerial talent at more junior levels to enhance localization- and succession-planning initiatives occurring within the organization.

Local junior managers with high potential were nominated to attend a two-day development center, designed and run by SHL in conjunction with trained-line and human resources managers from the organization. The development centers utilized a variety of different tests and exercises, including the OPQ, an in tray exercise, a presentation exercise, aptitude tests, a group exercise, the Test of Productive Thinking, and a competency-based career interview. All activities, except an aptitude test, were designed and conducted in Chinese.

The intervention involved more than 40 managers across a wide range of different regions in China, over one and a half years, and the results formed the basis of individual reports and feedback sessions for each manager. Also, the results were also built into the succession-planning model of the organization in China to establish which managers had the highest potential to reach what level(s) and within what kind of time period. This enabled the organization to plan for the cost-savings to be gained from localizing expatriate positions.

On the basis of the development center's results, each manager was equipped with a personal development plan that was reviewed and monitored by an individually assigned mentor. On a group basis, the developmental progress of the managers was reviewed at the regular quarterly meetings of the executive committee of the organization's senior management team in mainland China.

tional corporations and Western-run companies have incorporated psychometric assessment as part of their standard management practices worldwide; therefore, they request test data to support the large-scale recruitment and extensive organizational development that comprise an inevitable part of establishing new businesses in China. Thus, SHL has adapted for use in China tests related to aptitude and personality, as well as work simulation exercises, geared for assessment of fresh graduates and managerial applicants.

Another popular and large-scale area of psychological assessment involves screening of workers for start-up factories, typically using tests of mechanical aptitude, numeracy, and basic written English comprehension. Recently, SHL has worked with a mainland Chinese industrial-organizational psychologist in preparing materials for the mainland to increase the probability that translations will be equivalent linguistically, conceptually, and metrically.

SHL does not presently maintain an office in Taiwan. However, the company has plans to open one soon. Many of SHL's clients in Hong Kong and mainland China who also have operations in Taiwan typically request parallel assessments of staff in that location. Essentially, these are multinationals and financial institutions requesting assessments of customer service, and graduate-level and managerial staff measuring aptitudes, personality, and work simulations.

CASE STUDY 2

A multinational tobacco firm used the OPQ in China to help identify the preferences, styles, and behavior of its Chinese managers, in order to better identify training and development needs. The Chinese OPQ was used, which was designed and validated by an SHL China research and development team led by a Chinese organizational psychology professor on the mainland. A profile from the OPQ was produced against the China norm for each participant during a two-hour feedback discussion. On the basis of the profile and the feedback discussion, areas that managers could develop were identified and a personal development plan was constructed.

The focus was on the nature of the behavioral change required and the impact of the individual's personality style on the team, role, and job-fit in the context of the multinational's operations in China. An important advantage of the OPQ was that it profiles an individual's behavior in a work context situation; thus, in this situation, the OPQ allowed an exploration of the managers' potential based on their preferences and personality—information that was recorded for the purposes of succession planning for future roles.

Although SHL is the clear leader in occupational test development and supply within the region and, arguably, also worldwide, it's not alone in supplying and supporting test usage in greater China. The international firm PA Consultants has maintained an office in Hong Kong for over 20 years. PA promotes its own personality assessment instrument, the PA Personality Inventory (PAPI), which can be administered in English, as well as in both traditional and simplified Chinese characters. Assessing work roles and needs, the PAPI measures 20 scales grouped into seven cogent factors: (1) agreeableness, (2) seeking to achieve, (3) active dominance, (4) conscientious persistence, (5) openness to experience, (6) sociability, and (7) work tempo.

Deliberately avoiding the measurement of neurotic or psychotic features, the PAPI's item content and scales specifically focus on work-related concepts. The PAPI can be administered in two versions, both containing 90 items: (1) PAPI-N is a normative version used for comparing one person with another; (2) PAPI-I is an ipsative version, more suited to an individual assessment, such as looking at personal development.

Technical support for the ongoing development of the PAPI comes primarily from the firm's U.K.-based head office, which has recently launched a normative version of the PAPI to supplement the original nonnormative version. This is an important first step in raising the PAPI to the level of a credible pancultural psychometric instrument that can be reliably used for comparison of individuals across cultures. The PAPI is used predominantly by multinational corporations in China, Hong Kong, and Macao, for positions where comparison across cultures is desirable.

In addition to the PAPI, PA Consultants also supports the use in Hong Kong of a newly developed indigenous instrument, the Chinese Personality Assessment Inventory (CPAI). Professors Fannie Cheung and Leung Kwok at the Chinese University of Hong Kong have pioneered in developing this test. Dr. Cheung worked for many years on the translation and standardization of the Chinese version of the Minnesota Multiphasic Personality Inventory (MMPI). During the last 10 years, she turned her attention to the development of this new instrument, which attempts to measure both general personality and psychopathology.

Similar to the MMPI, the CPAI covers personality characteristics of normal, as well as clinical, populations. Measuring 35 scales in all, it encompasses 21 personality scales, 12 clinical scales, and 2 validity scales. The personality scales group into four underlying factors, including one factor—Chinese tradition—which measures a cluster of constructs specific to Chinese culture.

The CPAI was specifically developed to ensure near-perfect equivalence of the traditional and simplified character versions, a characteristic that few other instruments can claim. Extensive trailing of the CPAI in Hong Kong, China, Singapore, and Hawaii has confirmed the robustness of its psychometric properties and has significantly suggested the existence of a sixth personality dimension, interpersonal relatedness, over and above the Big Five factors (neuroticism, extraversion, openness, agreeableness, and conscientiousness) discussed in chapter 9, and demonstrated in numerous studies across a wide range of cultures.

This sixth dimension of personality among Chinese (i.e., interpersonal relatedness), captures orientation toward important characteristics of Chinese social relationships such as maintaining and saving face, seeking interpersonal harmony, and actively networking, and it highlights the potentially valuable contribution from locally developed, indigenous instruments toward increasing awareness and understanding of subtle cultural differences in personality and social behavior.

To date, the CPAI has been used mainly by local Chinese businesses for assessment of general-level employees in Hong Kong and Macao. PA Consultants has also supported the use of the CPAI by multinational clients in China for assessment of factory staff in start-up operations. PA Consultants does not have the exclusive right to sell the CPAI either in Hong Kong or in China; however, it is presently the major user of the CPAI in Hong Kong.

Professor Harry Hui of the University of Hong Kong has recently developed a second indigenous instrument. The Chinese Personality at Work (CPW) Questionnaire is a 225-item, work-context, forced-choice, self-report personality instrument structured after the Edwards Personal Preference schedule (EPPS). It measures 15 personality constructs similar to those used by the EPPS, although with refinements and additions that give weight to characteristics more typical of Chinese social and work behavior. Thus, it contains scales that assess nonabrasiveness, modesty, and introspectiveness. Validation studies of the instrument conducted in Hong Kong provide evidence of the CPW's value for predicting and explaining work behaviors of the Chinese, above and beyond contributions from pan-cultural instruments such as the NEO-PI-R.

For example, the job performance of Hong Kong real estate agents, measured by commission earned, is strongly associated with neuroticism and introversion as measured by the NEO-PI-R, highlighted previously in chapter 9. The meaning of this relationship is revealed by the additional finding that commission earned is also predicted by the CPW's scales of nonabrasiveness and modesty. It appears that neuroticism and introversion, largely regarded as negative personality traits in the West, may to some extent be associated with the positive Chinese traits of nonabrasiveness and modesty, which, at least in some work settings, can be associated with positive job performance. To date, the CPW has been used most extensively within Hong Kong businesses and service organizations, although a small number of multinational corporations have also utilized this instrument within China.

Several Western-developed personality measures are available for use with Chinese people in their local workplace. As mentioned, the NEO-PI-R has been trailed extensively around the world and has been translated into both traditional and simplified characters. At present, its use with Chinese people is mainly within the context of academic research, although at least one firm of human resources consultants in Hong Kong makes the instrument available for use by its clients. This test has the undeniable advantage that extensive research has affirmed its psychometric robustness. The multiple-language versions of the NEO-PI-R that exist seem to be highly equivalent, making direct comparisons among individuals from different cultures possible. There's also evidence that certain facets of the Big Five model—notably, the conscientiousness dimension—account for substantial variance in work performance across various industries. However, there remains skepticism in greater China and elsewhere that a broad, general-factor instrument that uses noncontextual items (e.g., the NEO-P-IR) can predict work behaviors as reliably as those that encompass work context items to measure multiple, narrow, work-related traits.

The Myers-Briggs Type Indicator (MBTI) is another Western-developed instrument that enjoys considerable popularity among the Chinese. An early version, Form G, has been translated into both traditional and simplified characters, and *Introduction to Type,* an important supplement explaining concepts relevant to the instrument, has also been translated into simplified characters. A more recent version, Form M, is currently being translated into traditional characters. Consulting Psychologists Press (CPP) in Palo Alto, California, holds the copyright to the MBTI, but Australian Psychologists Press (APP) in Melbourne, Australia, manages distribution of the Chinese versions.

Similar to its employment application in the United States, the MBTI is primarily used in training and development contexts, rather than in recruiting and selecting. Student counseling services at several of Hong Kong's tertiary institutions employ the instrument, and its popularity is increasing as a development tool within some of the larger Hong Kong financial institutions and transportation and service industries. The MBTI has also been trailed recently with managers and engineers in a joint venture enterprise in the Guangdong province of southern China, although according to APP, the Chinese government has banned legitimate distribution of the test within mainland China.

In summary, the use of psychometric instruments for screening, selection, promotion, and development is an important and growing feature of human resources management within greater China. Multinational organizations that operate in mainland China, Hong Kong, and Taiwan are likely to continue to demand Western-developed, pancultural instruments that allow near-equivalent assessment of individuals from and within diverse cultures around the globe. At the same time, continued research and development of local, indigenous instruments provide important resources for enhancing cross-cultural understanding and sensitivity. Though psychologists often seek to identify the universals of human behavior, when they are asked how these universals are expressed and interpreted within specific cultural contexts, they find ever-increasing cultural specificity. It seems that there will always be a place for both emic and etic approaches in the burgeoning field of employee assessment around the globe.

Glossary

The following terms are frequently used in the field of psychological testing today.

alternate form reliability   A major method of determining a test's *reliability*. Individuals are given alternate (i.e., highly similar but not identical) forms of the same test and their scores are compared.

aptitude test   A measure of individual ability in a specific domain, such as mechanical dexterity. These became important during the 1930s, particularly for vocational counseling and classifying industrial and military personnel.

attitude test   A psychological test that measures a person's attitudes in a particular domain, such as race relations or religion.

bell-shaped curve   See *normal distribution curve.*

construct validity   See *validity.* The extent to which a psychological test measures a theoretical construct or trait. Examples of such constructs are intelligence, verbal fluency, leadership ability, or anxiety.

content validity   Generally viewed as the most important method of determining *validity,* involving a systematic examination of test content to determine whether it covers a representative sample of the behavioral domain being measured. Achievement tests typically use this procedure.

criterion-related validity   See *validity.* A method of determining a test's validity by comparing its scores with a specified, usually real-life criterion. For example, scores on a test of mechanical aptitude might be compared with actual job performance ratings of mechanics.

extraversion See *introversion*. Refers to a person's tendency to gregariousness and nonsolitary activity.

five-factor (Big Five) model The most widely accepted current model of personality, encompassing the dimensions of neuroticism, extraversion, openness, conscientiousness, and agreeableness.

frequency distribution A statistical method of grouping scores into convenient class intervals and tallying each score in the appropriate interval.

group intelligence testing Group testing of intelligence was devised during World War I by the U.S. Army, under the direction of psychologist Robert Yerkes to process recruits as rapidly as possible.

integrity test A psychological test that measures a person's honesty. These are widely used in today's workplace.

interest test A psychological test that measures a person's interests, such as in various vocations or college majors.

intelligence testing The first scientific test of intelligence was developed in France by Alfred Binet and his associates in 1905. It was known as the Binet-Simon Scale and administered to children individually.

introversion A personality trait conceptualized by the Swiss psychiatrist Carl Jung, referring to an individual's tendency toward solitude and solitary activity. See *extraversion*.

ipsative test A psychological test in which an individual's scores are compared only with himself or herself, rather than on a continuum of high or low in comparison with others.

multiple-aptitude battery   See *aptitude test*. These are measures that assess a person's standing for several different traits, such as artistic, musical, and mechanical proficiency.

normal distribution curve   A statistical descriptor in which individuals' scores cluster near the center of the range and there is a gradual tapering-off of scores as the extremes are approached.

norms   The standardized scores on a given test, such as the percentage of individuals whose scores fall within a particular range.

percentile score   The percentage of individuals who score at a particular level, or within a particular range, on a test.

performance test   A form of personality measurement in which the individual has a task to perform whose purpose is generally disguised. The earliest versions of such tests were devised in the late 1920s and early 1930s to assess children's honesty.

personality test   A psychological measure of an individual's basic characteristics such as his or her attitudes, emotional adjustment, interests, interpersonal relations, and motivation. Personality tests were first widely used during World War I.

power test   A psychological test that has a time limit long enough for everyone to attempt all items. The difficulty of the items is steeply graded; contrasted with a *speed test*.

predictive validity   See *validity*. The extent to which a test predicts a person's subsequent success or failure in a given context based on his or her score.

projective tests   Favored especially by clinical psychologists to measure emotional adjustment, these measures present the individual with a relatively unstructured task that permits wide latitude in its solution. This might involve describing inkblots, making a drawing, or telling stories about presented pictures.

psychological tests These are essentially objective and standard-ized measures of a sample of behavior.

psychometrician A person who is trained in the field of psycho-metrics. This typically requires a doctorate in psychology with a strong background in statistics.

psychometrics The scientific field of constructing and validating psychological tests.

rating scale Among the oldest form of personality testing, in which individuals are presented with questions and asked to respond on a point scale concerning the degree of agreement or frequency of occurrence.

raw score A numerical score on a given test, meaningless without reference to the standardized norms for that test.

reliability Along with *validity,* the most important property of a psy-chological test. It refers to the consistency of scores obtained by the same individuals when reexamined with the same test on different occasions, or with different sets of equivalent items, or under other variable examining conditions.

scorer reliability A method of determining a test's *reliability,* in which two or more independent scorers rate an individual's responses. Such reliability is important in projective tests and tests of creativity, where responses are more difficult to categorize.

self-report inventory Among the most widely used forms of per-sonality testing, first developed by psychologist Robert Woodworth during World War I. The individual is asked to respond to a ques-tionnaire designed to measure such aspects as attitudes, interests, emotional adjustment, motivation, or social relations.

situational test See *performance test.*

speed test   A psychological test in which individual difference depends solely on speed of performance. Such a test is constructed with items of uniformly low difficulty; contrasted with power test.

split-half reliability   A method of determining reliability, in which a test is split into two halves that are administered at the same time, and individuals' scores on the two halves are then compared.

standardization   Referring to psychological tests, this term implies uniformity of procedure in administering and scoring.

standard deviation   A statistical measure of the variability of scores on a given test.

standard score   A raw score that is converted into a meaningful unit: specifically, the individual's distance from the mean in terms of the *standard deviation* on a given test.

standardized achievement tests   Spearheaded by the work of psychologist Edward Thorndike in the early 1900s, these measure scholastic attainment in such areas as arithmetic, reading recognition and comprehension, spelling, and writing proficiency. After World War II, such tests became an important admission criterion for colleges in the United States.

test-retest reliability   A major method of determining a test's *reliability*, the identical test is repeated on a second occasion and individuals' scores are compared.

validity   Generally regarded as the most important property of a psychological test. It refers to the issue of whether the test actually measures what it claims to measure. For example, does a questionnaire-format test of honesty actually measure a person's behavioral honesty in real life.

Bibliography

Adler, Seymour. "Personality and Work Behavior: Exploring the Linkages." *Applied Psychology: An International Review,* 45(3):207–224, 1996.

Anastasi, Anne. *Psychology Testing,* 7th ed. New York: Macmillan, 1988.

Arnold, Josh A., Sharon Arad, Jonathan A. Rhoades, and Fritz Drasgow. "The Empowering Leadership Questionnaire: The Construction and Validation of a New Scale for Measuring Leader Behaviors." *Journal of Organizational Behavior,* 21:249–269, 2000.

Arthur, Diane. *Workplace Testing: An Employer's Guide to Policies and Practices.* New York: American Management Association, 1994.

Ash, Philip. "Comparison of Two Integrity Tests Based Upon Youthful or Adult Attitudes and Experiences." *Journal of Business and Psychology,* 5(3):367–375, Spring 1991.

———. "Law and Regulation of Preemployment Inquiries." *Journal of Business and Psychology,* 5(3):291–300, Spring 1991.

Ashton, Michael C. "Personality and Job Performance: The Importance of Narrow Traits." *Journal of Organizational Behavior,* 19:289–303, 1998.

Aycan, Zynep. "Cross-Cultural Industrial and Organizational Psychology: Contributions, Past Developments, and Future Directions." *Journal of Cross-Cultural Psychology,* 31(1):110–128, January 2000.

Barnett, Tim, Winston N. McVea, and Kenneth Chadwick. "Preemployment questions under the Americans with Disabilities Act: An

Overview of the October 1995 EEOC Guidelines." *S.A.M. Advanced Management Journal,* 62(1):23–27, Winter 1997.

Baron, Robert A., and Gideon D. Markman. "Beyond Social Capital: How Social Skills Can Enhance Entrepreneurs' Success." *Academy of Management Executive,* 14(1):106–115, 2000.

Barrick, Murray R., and Michael K. Mount. "The Big Five Personality Dimensions and Job Performance: A Meta-Analysis." *Personnel Psychology,* 44:1–26, 1991.

——, and ——, "Effects of Impression Management and Self-Deception on the Predictive Validity of Personality Constructs." *Journal of Applied Psychology,* 81(3):261–272, 1996.

——, ——, and Judy P. Strauss. "Conscientiousness and Performance of Sales Representatives: Test of the Mediating Effects of Goal Setting." *Journal of Applied Psychology,* 78(5):712–722, 1993.

Bass, Bernard M. "Does the Transactional-Transformational Leadership Paradigm Transcend Organizational Boundaries?" *American Psychologist,* 5(2):130–139, February 1997.

——, and Bruce Avolio. *MLQ Multifactor Leadership Questionnaire.* Redwood City, CA: Mind Garden, 1995.

Bennis, Warren, and Burt Nanus. *Leaders: Strategies for Taking Charge,* 2nd ed. New York: Harper-Collins, 1997.

Beazley, Hamilton. "Meaning and Measurement of Spirituality in Organizational Settings: Development of a Spirituality Assessment Scale." *Dissertation Abstracts International Section A: Humanities and Social Sciences,* 58(12-A):4718, June 1998.

Black, J. Stewart, and Hal B. Gregersen. "The Right Way to Manage Expats." *Harvard Business Review,* 77(2):52–61, March-April 1997.

Black, Kimberli R. "Personality Screening in Employment." *American Business Law Journal,* 32(1):69–124, 1994.

Bloch, Deborah P., and Lee J. Richmond (eds.). *Connections Between Spirit and Work in Career Development.* Palo Alto, CA: Davies-Black, 1997.

Bosma, Hans, Stephen A. Stansfield, and Michael G. Marmot. "Job Control, Personal Characteristics, and Heart Disease." *Journal of Occupational Health Psychology,* 3(4):402–409, 1998.

Brewer, Geoffrey. "Shrink Rap: Is It Smart, or Just Plain Crazy to Use Psychological Tests When Hiring and Developing Employees?" *Sales and Marketing Management,* 147(9):28–33, September 1995.

Brown, Howard P., and John H. Peterson. "Assessing Spirituality in Addiction Treatment and Follow-Up: Development of the Brown-Peterson Recovery Progress Inventory (B-PRPI)." *Alcoholism Treatment Quarterly,* 8(2):21–45, 1991.

Butcher, James N., Jeeyoung Lim, and Elahe Nezami. "Objective Study of Abnormal Personality in Cross-Cultural Settings: The Minnesota Multiphasic Personality Inventory (MMPI-2)." *Journal of Cross-Cultural Psychology,* 29(1):189–211, January 1998.

Caird, Sally P. "What Do Psychological Tests Suggest about Entrepreneurs?" *Journal of Management Psychology,* 8(6):11–20, 1993.

Caldwell, David F., and Jerry M. Burger. "Personality Characteristics of Job Applicants and Success in Screening Interviews." *Personnel Psychology,* 51:119–136, 1998.

Caligiuri, Paula M. "The big five personality characteristics as predictors of expatriate's desire to terminate the assignment and supervisor-rated performance." *Personnel Psychology,* 53:67–88, Spring 2000.

Camara, Wayne J., and Dianne L. Schneider. "Integrity Tests: Facts and Unresolved Issues." *American Psychologist,* 94:112–119, February 1994.

Cappelli, Peter. "Career Jobs are Dead." *California Management Review,* 42(1):146–167, Fall 1999.

Carey, William B., and Sean McDevitt. *Coping with Children's Temperament.* New York: Basic Books, 1995.

Carless, Sally A., Alexander J. Wearing, and Leon Mann. "A Short Measure of Transformational Leadership." *Journal of Business and Psychology,* 14(3):389–405, Spring 2000.

Carlyn, Marcia. "An Assessment of the Myers-Briggs Type Indicator." *Journal of Personality Assessment,* 41(5):461–473, 1977.

Cash, Karen C., and George R. Gray. "A Framework for Accommodating Religion and Spirituality in the Workplace." *Academy of Management Executive,* 14(3):124–134, 2000.

Cavanaugh, Marcie R., Wendy R. Boswell, Mark V. Roehling, and John W. Boudreau. "An Empirical Examination of Self-Reported Work Stress among U.S. Managers." *Journal of Applied Psychology,* 85(1):65–74, 2000.

Cellar, Douglas F., Donna J. DeGrange DeGrendel, Jeffrey D. Klawsky, and Mark L. Miller. "The Validity of Personality, Service Orientation, and Reading Comprehension Measures as Predictors of Flight Attendant Training Performance." *Journal of Business and Psychology,* 11(1):43–58, Fall 1996.

Clapp, R. G., "Stability of Cognitive Style in Adults and Some Implications: A Longitudinal Study of the Kirton Adaptation-Innovation Inventory." *Psychological Reports,* 73:1235–1245, 1993.

Cook, Mark. *Personnel Selection and Productivity.* New York: Wiley, 1988.

Corbitt, J. Nathan. *Global Awareness Profile.* Yarmouth, ME: Intercultural Press, 1998.

Costa, Paul T., and Robert R. McRae. *Bibliography for the Revised NEO Personality Inventory (NEO PI-R) and NEO Five-Factor Inventory (NEO-FFI).* Odessa, FL: Psychological Assessment Resources, 1994.

———, and ———. *Manual Supplement for the NEO 4.* Odessa, FL: Psychological Assessment Resources, 1998.

Dakin, Stephen, V. Nilakant, and Ross Jensen. "The Role of Personality Testing in Managerial Selection." *Journal of Managerial Psychology*, 9(5):3–11, 1994.

Daley, Amanda J., and Gaynor Parfitt. "Good Health—Is It Worth It? Mood States, Physical Well-Being, Job Satisfaction and Absenteeism in Members and Non-Members of a British Corporate Health and Fitness Club." *Journal of Occupational and Organizational Psychology*, 69:121–134, 1996.

Dalton, Maxine, and Meena Wilson. "The Relationship of the Five-Factor Model of Personality to Job Performance for a Group of Middle Eastern Expatriate Managers." *Journal of Cross-Cultural Psychology*, 31(2):250–258, March 2000.

DeFrank, Richard S., Robert Konopaske, and John M. Ivancevich. "Executive Travel Stress: Perils of the Road Warrior." *Academy of Management Executive*, 14(2):58–71, 2000.

Digman, John M. "Personality Structure: Emergence of the Five-Factor Model." *Annual Review of Psychology*, 41:417–440, 1990.

"Do Your Job-Applicant Tests Make the Grade?" *Personnel Journal*, 75(8):16–17, August 1996 (Supplement).

Dulewicz, Victor, and Peter Herbert. "Predicting Advancement to Senior Management from Competencies and Personality Data: A Seven-Year Follow-Up Study." *British Academy of Management*, 10:13–22, 1999.

———, and Malcolm Higgs. "Soul Researching." *People Management*, unpaged, October 1998.

———, and ———. "Can Emotional Intelligence be Measured and Developed?" *Leadership and Organization Development Journal*, 20(5):242–252, 1999.

———, and ———. "Emotional Intelligence: Managerial Fad or Valid Construct?" *Journal of Managerial Psychology*, in press.

————, and ————. "A Study of 360 Degree Assessment of Emotional Intelligence." *Selection and Development Review*, in press.

Dworkin, Terry Morehead. "Protecting Private Employees from Enhanced Monitoring: Legislative Approaches." *American Business Law Journal*, 28(1):59–86, Spring 1990.

Ebrahimi, Bahman P. "Motivation to Manage in Hong Kong: Modification and Test of Miner Sentence Completion Scale-H." *Journal of Managerial Psychology*, 12(6):404–414, 1997.

Ellison, Craig W., and Joel Smith. "Toward an Integrative Measure of Health and Well-Being." *Journal of Psychology and Theology*, 19(1):35–48, 1991.

Farmer, Richard, and Norman D. Sundberg. "Boredom-Proneness—The Development and Correlates of a New Scale." *Journal of Personality Assessment*, 50(1):4–17, 1986.

Feldman, Daniel C., and Mark C. Bolino. "Careers Within Careers: Reconceptualizing the Nature of Career Anchors and Their Consequences." *Human Resource Management Review*, 6(2):89–112, 1996.

Fernandez-Araoz, Claudio. "Hiring Without Firing." *Harvard Business Review*, 109–120, July-August 1999.

Fogelman, Dannie B. "Minimizing the Risk of Violence in the Workplace." *Employment Relations Today*, 83–93, Spring 2000.

Forrest, Linda. "Career Assessment for Couples." *Journal of Employment Counseling*, 31(4):168–188, December 1994.

Forster, Nick. "Expatriates and the Impact of Cross-Cultural Training." *Human Resource Management Journal*, 10(3):63–78, 2000.

Frost, Alan G., and Fred M. Rafilson. "Overt Integrity Tests Versus Personality-Based Measures of Delinquency: An Empirical Comparison." *Journal of Business and Psychology*, 3(3):269–277, Spring 1989.

Goldberg, Lewis R. "An Alternative Description of Personality," *Journal of Personality and Social Psychology,* 59(6):1216–1229, 1990.

———. "The Structure of Personality Traits." *American Psychologist,* 48(1):26–34, January 1993.

Goleman, Daniel. *Emotional Intelligence.* New York: Bantam, 1995.

———. *Working with Emotional Intelligence.* New York: Bantam, 2000.

Goodstein, Leonard D., and Richard I. Lanyon. "Applications of Personality Assessment to the Workplace: A Review." *Journal of Business and Psychology,* 13(3):291–319, Spring 1999.

Greengard, Samuel. "Are You Well-Armed to Screen Applicants?" *Personnel Journal,* 74:84–93, December 1995.

Haney, Walter M., George F. Madaus, and Robert Lyons. *The Fractured Market for Standardized Testing.* Boston: Kluwer Academic Publishers, 1993.

Harris, Julie Aitken, Robert Saltstone, and Maryann Fraboni. "An Evaluation of the Job Stress Questionnaire with a Sample of Entrepreneurs." *Journal of Business and Psychology,* 13(3):447–455, Spring 1999.

Harvey, Robert J., and William D. Murry. "Scoring the Myers-Briggs Type Indicator: Empirical Comparison of Preference Score Versus Latent-Trait Methods." *Journal of Personality Assessment,* 62(1):116–129, 1994.

Harville, Donald L. "Employment Test Usage as a Predictor of Gross Domestic Product." *Journal of Business and Psychology,* 11(3):399–408, Spring 1997.

Hoffman, Edward. *The Drive for Self: Alfred Adler and the Founding of Individual Psychology.* Reading, MA: Addison-Wesley, 1994.

——— (ed.). *Future Visions: The Unpublished Papers of Abraham Maslow.* Thousand Oaks, CA: Sage, 1996.

————. *The Right to Be Human: A Biography of Abraham Maslow,* 2d ed. New York: McGraw-Hill, 1999.

————. *Ace the Corporate Personality Test.* New York: McGraw-Hill, 2000.

Hogan, Robert, and Rex Blake. "John Holland's Vocational Typology and Personality Theory." *Journal of Vocational Behavior,* 5:41–56, 1999.

————, and Joyce Hogan. *Hogan Personality Inventory Manual,* 2nd ed. Tulsa, OK: Hogan Assessment Systems, 1995.

Hough, Leatta M. "The Millennium for Personality Psychology: New Horizons or Good Old Daze." *Applied Psychology: An International Review,* 47(2):233–261, 1997.

Howard, Pierce J., and Jane Howard. "Buddy, Can You Paradigm?" *Training and Development,* 49(9):28–39, September 1995.

Hunt, Steven T. "Generic Work Behavior: An Investigation into the Dimensions of Entry-Level, Hourly Job Performance." *Personnel Psychology,* 49:51–83, 1996.

Hutri, Merja. "When Careers Reach a Dead End: Identification of Occupational Crisis States." *Journal of Psychology,* 130:383–399, July 1996.

Jeannert, Richard, and Rob Silzer (eds.). *Individual Psychological Assessment.* San Francisco: Jossy-Bass, 1998.

Johnson, Pamela J. "Teacher Wins Ruling over College Chief." *Los Angeles Times, Ventura County Edition,* Part B, p. 1, September 25, 1998.

Jones, John W. "Assessing Privacy Invasiveness of Psychological Test Items: Job Relevant Versus Clinical Measures of Integrity." *Journal of Business and Psychology,* 5(4):531–535, Summer 1991.

Judge, Timothy A., Chad Higgins, Carl J. Thoresen, and Murray R. Barrick. "The Big Five Personality Traits, General Mental Ability, and Career Success Across the Life Span." *Personnel Psychology,* 52:621–652, 1999.

————, Joseph J. Martocchio, and Carl J. Thoresen. "Five-Factor Model of Personality and Employee Absence." *Journal of Applied Psychology*, 82(5):745–755, 1997.

Kanfer, Ruth, Phillip L. Ackerman, Todd Murtha, and Maynard Goff. "Personality and Intelligence in Industrial and Organizational Psychology. In Donald H. Saklofske and Moshe Zeidner (eds.), *International Handbook of Personality and Intelligence*. New York: Plenum, 1995.

Kass, Jared D., Richard Friedman, Jane Leserman, Patricia C. Zuttermeister, and Herbert Benson. "Health Outcomes and a New Index of Spiritual Experience." *Journal for the Scientific Study of Religion*, 30(1):203–211, 1991.

Kelley, Colleen, and Judith Meyers. *Cross-Cultural Adaptability Inventory Manual*. Minneapolis, MN: National Computer Systems, 1995.

Kelley, Patrick L., Rick R. Jacobs, and James Farr. "Effects of Multiple Administrations of the MMPI for Employee Screening." *Personnel Psychology*, 47(3):575–592, Autumn 1994.

Kirton, Michael J. (ed.). *Adaptors and Innovators: Styles of Creativity and Problem-Solving*. London, UK: Routledge, 1994.

Kobbs, Steven W., and Richard D. Arvey. "Distinguishing Deviant and Non-Deviant Nurses Using the Personnel Reaction Blank." *Journal of Business and Psychology*, 8(2):255–264, Winter 1993.

Kolbe, Kathy. *Pure Instinct: Business' Untapped Resource*. New York: Times Books, 1993.

Kolbe, Kathy. *The Conative Connection: Exploring the Link Between Who You Are and How You Perform*. Reading, MA: Addison-Wesley, 1990.

Kroeger, Otto, and Janet Thuesen. *Type Talk at Work: How the 16 Personality Types Determine Your Success on the Job*. New York: Dell, 1992.

Laden, Vicki A., and Gregory Schwartz. "Psychiatric Disabilities, the Americans with Disabilities Act, and the New Workplace Violence Account." *Berkeley Law Journal*, 246–270, 2000.

Lambing, Peggy, and Charles Kuehl. *Entrepreneurship.* New York: Prentice-Hall, 1997.

Lasson, Elliot D., and Alan R. Bass. "Integrity Testing and Deviance: Construct Validity Issues and the Role of Situational Factors." *Journal of Business and Psychology,* 12(2):121–145, Winter 1997.

Leclerc, Gilbert, Richard Lefrancois, Micheline Dube, Rejean Hebert, and Philippe Gaulin. "Criterion Validity of a New Measure of Self-Actualization." *Psychological Reports,* 85:1167–1176, 1999.

Lefrancois, Richard, Gilbert Leclerc, Micheline Dube, Rejean Hebert, and Philippe Gaulin. "Reliability of a New Measure of Self-Actualization." *Psychological Reports,* 82:875–878, 1998.

Lemann, Nicholas. *The Big Test: The Secret History of the American Meritocracy.* New York: Farrar, Straus and Giroux, 1999.

Leong, Frederick T. L., Beryl L. Hesketh, and Mark L. Savickas. "Guest Editors' Introduction—International Perspectives on Vocational Psychology." *Journal of Vocational Behavior,* 52:271–274, 1998.

LoBello, Steven G., and Benjamin Sims. "Fakability of a Commercially Produced Pre-Employment Integrity Test." *Journal of Business and Psychology,* 8(2):265–273, Winter 1993.

Loevinger, Jane. "Has Psychology Lost its Conscience?" *Journal of Personality Assessment,* 62(1):2–8, 1994.

"Long Hours May Be Hazardous to Your Health." *Worklife,* 12(2):4–5, 1999.

Mael, Fred A., Mary Connerley, and Ray A. Morath. "None of your Business: Parameters of Biodata Invasiveness." *Personnel Psychology,* 49:614–650, 1996.

Manese, Wilfredo R. *Fair and Effective Employment Testing.* New York: Quorum, 1986.

Martin, Phyllis. "Hire Smart, Hire Right: The Artful Interview." *Working Woman,* 71–76, March 1989.

Martin, Scott L., and Crystal Godsey. "Assessing the Validity of a Theoretically-Based Substance Abuse Scale for Personnel Selection." *Journal of Business and Psychology*, 13(3):323–337, Spring 1999.

Maslach, Christine, Susan E. Jackson, and Michael Leiter. *Maslach Burnout Inventory Manual*. Palo Alto, CA: Consulting Psychologists Press, 1996.

Matteson, Michael, and John Ivancevich. *Managing Job Stress and Health*. New York: The Free Press, 1992.

McDaniel, Michael A. "Applicant-Faking Stories: Volume 1." *Industrial-Organizational Psychologist*, 20:13–14, 1999.

McLelland, David C. *The Achieving Society*. Princeton, NJ: Van Nostrand, 1961.

McManus, Margaret A., and Mary L. Kelly. "Personality Measures and Biodata: Evidence Regarding their Incremental Predictive Value in the Life Insurance Industry." *Personnel Psychology*, 52:137–148, 1999.

Medcof, John W., and Peter A. Hausdorf. "Instruments to Measure Opportunities to Satisfy Needs, and Degree of Satisfaction of Needs, in the Workplace." *Journal of Occupational and Organizational Psychology*, 68:193–208, 1995.

Mignin, Robert J., Joan E. Gale, and Pamela Davidson. "Workplace Stress Claims: What Is the Employer's Responsibility?" *Employee Relations Law Journal*, 25(2):109–118, Autumn 1999.

Meijer, Rob R. "Consistency of Test Behavior and Individual Difference in Precision of Prediction." *Journal of Occupational Psychology*, 71:147–160, 1998.

Miner, John B. *Miner Sentence Completion Test*. Buffalo, NY: Organizational Measurement Systems Press, 1981.

———. *Scoring Guide for the Miner Sentence Completion Test, Form P.* Atlanta, GA: Organizational Measurement Systems, 1981.

————. *Scoring Guide for the Miner Sentence Completion Test, Form T.* Atlanta, GA: Organizational Measurement Systems Press, 1986.

————. "Entrepreneurs, High Growth Entrepreneurs, and Managers: Contrasting and Overlapping Motivational Patterns." *Journal of Business Venturing,* 5:221–234, 1990.

————. *The Four Routes to Entrepreneurial Success.* San Francisco: Berrett-Koehler, 1996.

————. "The Expanded Horizon for Achieving Entrepreneurial Success." *Organizational Dynamics,* 25(3):54–68, Winter 1997.

————. "A Psychological Typology and Its Relationship to Entrepreneurial Success." *Entrepreneurship and Regional Development,* 9:319–334, 1997.

————, and Michael H. Capps. *How Honesty Testing Works.* Westport, CT: Quorum, 1996.

————, Chao-Chuan Chen, and K. C. Yu. "Theory Testing Under Adverse Conditions: Motivation to Manage in the People's Republic of China." *Journal of Applied Psychology,* 76(3):343–349, 1991.

————, Norman R. Smith, and Jeffrey Braker. "Role of Entrepreneurial Task Motivation in the Growth of Technologically Innovative Firms: Interpretations from Follow-Up Data." *Journal of Applied Psychology,* 79(4):627–630, 1994.

Minor, Marianne. *Preventing Workplace Violence: Positive Management Strategies.* Menlo Park, CA: Crisp, 1995.

Mitchell, Clifton W., and I. Michael Shuff. "Personality Characteristics of Hospice Volunteers as Measured by Myers-Briggs Type Indicator." *Journal of Personality Assessment,* 65(3):521–532, 1995.

Mitroff, Ian I., and Elizabeth Denton. "A Study of Spirituality in the Workplace." *Sloan Management Review,* 83–92, Summer 1999.

Moad, Jeff. "Psych Tests for MIS Staff: Is This Nuts?" *Datamation,* 40(13):27–29, 1 July 1994.

Mumford, Michael D. "Construct Validity and Background Data: Issues, Abuses, and Future Directions." *Human Resource Management Review,* 9(2):117–136, Summer 1999.

Murphy, Emmett. *Leadership: The Groundbreaking Program to Develop and Improve Your Leadership Ability.* New York: Wiley, 1996.

Nanus, Burt. *Visionary Leadership.* San Francisco: Jossey-Bass, 1992.

Narayanan, Lakshmi, Shanker Menon, and Edward L. Levine. "Personality Structure: A Culture-Specific Examination of the Five-Factor Model." *Journal of Personality Assessment,* 64(1):51–62, 1995.

Nass, Clifford. "Computer-Synthesized Speech and Personality." *Journal of Experimental Psychology-Applied,* in press.

Ni, Yuching, and Neil M. A. Hauenstein. "Applicant Reactions to Personality Tests: Effects of Item Invasiveness and Face Validity." *Journal of Business and Psychology,* 12(4):391–406, Summer 1998.

Nichols, David S., and Roger L. Greene. "Dimensions of Deception in Personality Assessment: The Example of the MMPI-2." *Journal of Personality Assessment,* 68(2):251–266, 1997.

Niehoff, Brian P., and Robert J. Paul. "Causes of Employee Theft and Strategies that HR Managers Can Use for Prevention." *Human Resource Management,* 39(1):51–64, Spring 2000.

Nordvik, Hilmar. "Relationships Between Holland's Vocational Typology, Schein's Career Anchors and Myers-Briggs Types." *Journal of Occupational and Organizational Psychology,* 69:263–275, 1996.

Ones, Deniz S., and Chockalingham Viswesvaran. "The Effects of Social Desirability and Faking on Personality and Integrity Assessment for Personnel Selection." *Human Performance,* 11(2/3):245–269, 1998.

———, and ———. "Gender, Age, and Race Differences on Overt Integrity Tests: Results Across Four Large-Scale Job Applicant Data Sets." *Journal of Applied Psychology,* 83(1):35–42, 1998.

O'Roark, Ann M. "Comment on Cowan's Interpretation of the Myers-Briggs Type Indicator and Jung's Psychological Functions." *Journal of Personality Assessment,* 55(3,4):815–817, 1990.

Osipow, Samuel H. *Occupational Stress Inventory, Revised Edition, Professional Manual.* Palo Alto, CA: Consulting Psychologists Press, 1998.

Parnell, John A. "Improving the Fit Between Organizations and Employees." *S.A.M. Advanced Management Journal,* 63(1):35–42, Winter 1998.

Potosky, Denise, and Philip Bobko. "Computer Versus Paper-and-Pencil Administration Mode and Response Distortion in Noncognitive Selection Tests." *Journal of Applied Psychology,* 82(2):293–299, 1997.

Piedmont, Ralph L. *The Revised NEO Personality Inventory: Clinical and Research Applications.* New York: Plenum, 1998.

Piedmont, Ralph L., and Joon-Ho Chae. "Cross-Cultural Generalizability of the Five-Factor Model of Personality: Development and Validation of the NEO PI-R for Koreans." *Journal of Cross-Cultural Psychology,* 28(2):131–155, March 1997.

Quenk, Naomi L. *Essentials of Myers-Briggs Type Indicator Assessment.* New York: Wiley, 2000.

Quick, James Campbell. "Introduction to the Measurement of Stress at Work." *Journal of Occupational Health Psychology,* 3(4):291–293, 1998.

Raymark, Patrick H., Mark J. Schmit, and Robert M. Guion. "Identifying Potentially Useful Personality Constructs for Employee Selection." *Personnel Psychology,* 50:723–736, 1997.

Renesch, John. *Leadership in a New Era: Visionary Approaches to the Biggest Crisis of our Time.* San Francisco: Sterling and Stone, 1994.

Rentsch, Joan, and Scott Hutchison. "Testing the Test." *HRFocus,* 13, March 1999.

Richardson, Peter Tufts. *Four Spiritualities: Expressions of Self, Expressions of Spirit.* Palo Alto, CA: Davies-Black, 1996.

Rogers, Timothy B. *The Psychological Testing Enterprise.* Pacific Grove, CA: Brooks/Cole, 1995.

Rosse, Joseph G., Howard E. Miller, and Laurie Keitel Barnes. "Combining Personality and Cognitive Ability Predictors for Hiring Service-Oriented Employees." *Journal of Business and Psychology,* 5(4):431–445, Summer 1991.

Ryan, Ann Marie, and Marja Lasek. "Negligent Hiring and Defamation: Areas of Liability Related to Pre-Employment Inquiries." *Personnel Psychology,* 44:313–325, 1991.

———, Robert E. Ployhart, Gary J. Greguras, and Mark J. Schmit. "Test Preparation Programs in Selection Contexts: Self-Selection and Program Effectiveness." *Personnel Psychology,* 51:599–620, 1998.

———, Mark J. Schmit, Diane L. Daum, Stephane Brutus, Sheila A. McCormick, and Michelle Haff Brodke. "Workplace Integrity: Differences in Perceptions of Behaviors and Situational Factors." *Journal of Business and Psychology,* 12(1):67–83, Fall 1997.

Sackett, Paul R., and Janet Wanek. "New Developments in the Use of Measures of Honesty, Integrity, Conscientiousness, Dependability, Trustworthiness, and Reliability for Personnel Selection." *Personnel Psychology,* 49:787–826, 1996.

Saklofske, Donald H., and Moshe Zeidner (eds.). *International Handbook of Personality and Intelligence.* New York: Plenum, 1998.

Salgado, Jesus F. "The Five Factor Model of Personality and Job Performance in the European Community." *Journal of Applied Psychology,* 82:30–43, 1997.

Sampson, James P. "Using the Internet to Enhance Testing in Counseling." *Journal of Counseling and Development,* 78:348–356, Summer 2000.

Saunders, Frances Wright. *Katharine and Isabel: Mothers's Light, Daughter's Journey.* Palo Alto, CA: Consulting Psychologists Press, 1991.

Schnell, Eugene R. *The Leadership Report Using FIRO-B and MBTI: Coach's Guide.* Palo Alto, CA: Consulting Psychologists Press, 1999.

Schoenfeldt, Lyle F. "From Dust Bowl Empiricism to Rational Constructs in Biographical Data." *Human Resource Management Review,* 9(2):147–167, 1999.

Schwartz, Shalom H. "A Theory of Cultural Values and Some Implications for Work." *Applied Psychology: An International Review,* 48(1):23–47, 1999.

Segel, Jonathan A. "When Charles Manson Comes to the Workplace." *HR Magazine,* 39(6):33–38, June 1994.

Shostrom, Everett L. *Personal Orientation Manual: An Inventory for the Measurement of Self-Actualization.* San Diego, CA: Educational and Industrial Testing Service, 1974.

Silver, A. David. *The Entrepreneurial Life: How to Go for It and Get It.* New York: Wiley, 1983.

Smith, Timothy W. "Punt, Pass and Ponder the Questions: In the N.F.L., Personality Tests Help Teams Judge the Draftees." *New York Times,* 11–12, 20 April 1997.

Snell, Andrea F., Eric J. Sydell, and Sarah B. Lueke. "Towards a Theory of Applicant Faking: Integrating Studies Of Deception." *Human Resource Management Review,* 9(2):219–242, 1999.

Solomon, Charlene Manner. "Testing at Odds with Diversity Efforts?" *Personnel Journal,* 75(4):131–140, April 1996.

Spirrison, Charles L. "Factorial Hue and Cry: Comments On Jane Loevinger's 'Has Psychology Lost its Conscience?' " *Journal of Personality Assessment,* 63(3):579–583, 1994.

Spragins, Ellyn E. "Psychological Tests: Inside Straight." *Inc.,* 15(1):34–35, January 1993.

Standard, Rebecca P., Daya S. Sandhu, and Linda C. Painter. "Assessment of Spirituality in Counseling." *Journal of Counseling and Development*, 78:204–210, Spring 2000.

Starkey, Malcolm. "Testing the Tests." *Management Today*, 76–79, May 1992.

Steiner, Dirk D., and Stephen W. Gilliland. "Fairness Reaction to Personnel Selection Techniques in France and the United States." *Journal of Applied Psychology*, 81(2):134–141, 1996.

Sternberg, Robert J., and Patricia Ruzgis. *Personality and Intelligence.* Cambridge, England: Cambridge University Press, 1994.

Stone, Dianna L. "Perceived Fairness of Biodata as a Function of the Purpose of the Request for Information and Gender of the Applicant." *Journal of Business and Psychology*, 11(3):313–323, Spring 1997.

———, and Gwen Jones. "Perceived Fairness of Biodata as a Function of the Purpose of the Request for Information and Gender of the Applicant." *Journal of Business and Psychology*, 11(3):313–323, Spring 1997.

The Stanton Survey: New Edition. Charlotte, NC: Pinkerton Service Group, 1995.

Thompson, James W. "An Internal Validation of London House's Step Battery." *Journal of Business and Psychology*, 9(1):81–89, Fall 1994.

Thoms, Peg, and David B. Grenberger. "A Test of Vision Training and Potential Antecedents to Leaders' Visioning Ability." *Human Resource Development Quarterly*, 9(1):3–19, Spring 1998.

Thomson, Lenore. *Personality Type: An Owner's Manual.* Boston: Shambhala, 1998.

Thorne, B. Michael, Julia Houston Fyfe, and Thomas G. Caskadon. "The Myers-Briggs Type Indicator and Coronary Heart Disease." *Journal of Personality Assessment*, 51(4):545–554, 1987.

Tieger, Paul D., and Barbara-Barron Tieger. *Do What You Are: Discover the Perfect Career for You Through the Secrets of Personality Type,* 2nd ed. Boston: Little, Brown, 1995.

Tierney, Pamela, Steven M. Farmer, and George B. Graen. "An Examination of Leadership and Employee Creativity: The Relevance of Traits and Relationships." *Personnel Psychology,* 52:591–619, 1999.

Tokar, David M., Ann R. Fischer, and Linda Mezydlo Subich. "Personality and Vocational Behavior: A Selective Review of the Literature, 1993–1997." *Journal of Vocational Behavior,* 53:115–153, 1998.

Turkington, Carol A. *Stress Management for Busy People.* New York: McGraw-Hill, 1998.

Tyler, Kathryn. "Put Applicants' Skills to the Test." *HR Magazine,* 75–80, January 2000.

Ueda, Yoshikazu. "A Study of the Concept of the Healthy Personality." *Japanese Health Psychology,* 2:1–13, 1993.

Vagg, Peter R., and Charles D. Spielberger. "Occupational Stress: Measuring Job Pressure and Organizational Support in the Workplace." *Journal of Occupational Health Psychology,* 3(4):294–305, 1998.

Waterman, Judith A., and Jenny Rogers. *Introduction to the FIRO-B.* Palo Alto, CA: Consulting Psychologists Press, 1996.

Weisberg, Daniel. "Preparing for the Unthinkable." *Management Review,* 83(3):58–60, March 1994.

Weisinger, Hendrie. *Anger at Work: Learning the Art of Anger Management on the Job.* New York: Morrow, 1995.

Ziyal, Leyula. "The Single Psychological Test: (Or Test System) Measuring for Hope." *Journal of Managerial Psychology,* 6(2):21–24, 1991.

Index of Psychological Tests

Index

About the Author

Edward Hoffman, Ph.D., is the critically acclaimed author of *The Right to Be Human: A Biography of Abraham Maslow* (McGraw-Hill), *The Drive for Self,* and *Future Visions: The Unpublished Papers of Abraham Maslow.* A licensed clinical psychologist based in New York City, he has over 20 years of professional experience with an emphasis on psychological evaluation, and lectures widely throughout the United States, Europe, South America, and Asia.